THE MEXICANS IN OKLAHOMA

by Michael M. Smith

University of Oklahoma Press
Norman

*Oklahoma Image is a project sponsored by the
Oklahoma Department of Libraries
and the Oklahoma Library Association,
and made possible by a grant from the
National Endowment for the Humanities.*

Library of Congress Cataloging in Publication Data

Smith, Michael M.
 The Mexicans in Oklahoma.

 (Newcomers to a new land)
 Bibliography: p.
 1. Mexican Americans — Oklahoma — History.
 2. Oklahoma — History. I. Title. II. Series.
 F705.M5S63   976.6'0046872   79-6717

CONTENTS

To Susana, Marisol, Adriana, and Michael

PREFACE

In many respects, Mexicans have been Oklahoma's "invisible minority." Authors of state histories, journal articles, and ethnic studies have overlooked their role—indeed, their very presence—in the state. This short book, focusing on the first generation, is intended to be an introduction to the Mexican experience in Oklahoma. Perhaps this study will encourage others to examine more carefully Mexican contributions to the state's economic development and cultural heritage.

For their assistance in completing this work, I wish to thank Kay Fagin and the Oklahoma Image staff; the three editors of the "Newcomers to a New Land" series, H. Wayne Morgan, Douglas D. Hale, and Rennard Strickland; the members of the Documents and Social Sciences divisions of the Oklahoma State University Edmond Low Library; and the personnel of the Oklahoma Historical Society.

Aurora and Jack Helton, Dr. Edward Esparza, Rosa King, Anita Martínez, Father Louis Scagnelli, Father John Michael Payne, Tomás Silva, Sister Kathleen Blanchard, Father Ward Darnell, Sister Silvia Negrete, Francisco Hernández, and Joe Columbus provided encouragement and cooperation during the course of this study.

I extend my deepest gratitude to Gregorio Martínez, Simeón and Sofía Urende, Heginio Casillas, Agustín and Dolores Romero, Guadalupe Nieto, Paul Leyja, Silvia Torres, Raymond and María Coronado, Petra Martínez, and Miguel González. They opened their homes and their hearts and shared their lives with me. In a large measure, this is their story.

For reasons only they can truly appreciate, I thank my family—Susana, Marisol, Adriana, and Michael.

Oklahoma State University   *Michael M. Smith*

Chapter 1

OKLAHOMA AND MEXICO: A DISTANT RELATIONSHIP

Oklahoma lies just beyond the vast geo-cultural region historically designated as the Spanish Borderlands—that part of the American Southwest which today clearly manifests the physical, cultural, and linguistic legacy of its Spanish-Mexican past. Direct Mexican influence in Oklahoma, compared with that in Texas, New Mexico, Arizona, or California, has been minimal. Yet, from 1541, when the first Spanish *conquistadores* reached the Great Plains and crossed western Oklahoma seeking the fabled riches of Gran Quivira, until the early twentieth century, when thousands of Mexican immigrants seeking simple economic survival entered the young state, Mexico and Oklahoma shared an intermittent, albeit subtle, relationship.

In the late spring of 1541, Spanish soldiers under the command of Francisco Vásquez de Coronado became the first Europeans to enter Oklahoma. They came from Mexico. More than a year before, Coronado assembled an army at Compostela, on the Pacific coast in the northwestern province of New Galicia. Over three hundred Spaniards eagerly awaited the *entrada* into the mysterious reaches of northern New Spain, as Mexico was then called. Their goal was the fabulous Seven Cities of Cíbola, where buildings were made of pure gold, doors studded with turquoise, and whole streets filled with the shops of goldsmiths who produced marvelous objects of the coveted metal.

This expedition was the most impressive ever assembled in the newly conquered land. Antonio de Mendoza, Viceroy of Mexico, had traveled from Mexico City to extend his personal best wishes on the venture. Horsemen, whose brightly polished armor and lances flashed in the sun, were astride the finest mounts in the land. Foot soldiers, some with shields and swords, bore crossbows and arquebuses. A

1

thousand Indian allies, their bodies striped with red, yellow, and black paint, had been conscripted to join the venture. The viceroy provided mules, cannons, and a thousand horses at royal expense. Hundreds of cattle, sheep, goats, and pigs would comprise a commissary on the hoof. At the head of this magnificent entourage rode Coronado in his glimmering golden armor and Marcos de Niza, a grey-robed Franciscan friar.

In 1539 Fray Marcos reported seeing the first of the Seven Cities, although admittedly only at a distance from a high plateau. The tale of what Fray Marcos thought he saw inspired the Spaniards to risk their lives and win their fortunes. In July 1540, however, when Coronado and his men reached the site of Cíbola in present-day southeastern Arizona, they found nothing more than a poor Zuñi pueblo (Hawikuh) made of adobe. The Spaniards sacked the city but found no gold, silver, or precious jewels. To protect Fray Marcos from the soldiers, who cursed him for his "lies," Coronado sent him and a small escort back to Mexico City to report to Mendoza.

Disillusioned, weary, and hungry, the Spaniards took new heart after encountering El Turco, a slave held by the Indians. El Turco, probably a Pawnee, told the Spaniards about Gran Quivira—his homeland—which lay to the east. He added that beyond Quivira they would find a river two leagues wide, where the fish were bigger than horses. Natives plied the river in canoes that bore gold figureheads and oarlocks. Tatarax, king of this land, reposed under a huge tree that was adorned with gold bells whose music lulled him into a pleasant sleep. Even the lowliest servants ate and drank from utensils of pure gold. If what El Turco had told them was accurate, the Spaniards believed that Gran Quivira must be the richest place yet discovered in the New World.

In April 1541, the irresistible image of Gran Quivira lured the Spaniards onto the Great Plains. They traveled for weeks across the flat, dry land. Food ran short, the horses weakened, and the men constantly grumbled. Coronado decided to send his main army back to Tiguex, near present-day Albuquerque. Choosing thirty men and the best mounts, Coronado continued north, moved through what became the Texas and Oklahoma panhandles, crossed the Arkansas River, and finally reached Gran Quivira, near present-day Great Bend, Kansas. Again the Spaniards were disappointed. Gran Quivira was only a miserable Wichita Indian village of mud, stick, and thatch huts. Disconsolate, Coronado reported to King Carlos V that the people of Gran Quivira were as barbarous as any he had encountered in his arduous journey. There was no gold or any other precious metal in that region. The enraged Spaniards strangled El Turco for his duplicity and a few weeks later returned to Mexico. Defeated by the forbidding plains and constant hardship, Coronado took little solace in the fact that he and the members of his expedition had discovered the Grand Canyon and the Continental Divide and had completed one of the greatest land expeditions in modern times.

After Coronado's disappointing experience, few Spaniards returned to the Great Plains. Part of an expedition under the command of Hernando de Soto, who led a nearly simultaneous *entrada* from Florida, may have reached as far as the Grand River in northeastern Oklahoma in 1542. In 1601, while leading an expedition from New Mexico to Gran Quivira, Juan de Oñate crossed the Canadian River in Oklahoma. Except for a few scattered reminders, however, there was little visible evidence of the *conquistadores'* presence in Oklahoma.

A variety of factors forestalled Spanish settlement and exploitation of the Great Plains. The land itself, an immense verdant ocean of waving grass, discouraged and disoriented the traveler. The country over which the buffalo ponderously traveled was so flat that one could see the sky between the animals' legs. Spaniards erected stacks of bones and dung to mark a trail because there were no stones or trees. Men became lost if they strayed but half a league and would wander for days trying to find their way back to camp. The Spaniards found no gold or silver. There were no docile, populous sedentary Indian civilizations whose souls they could convert or whose labor they could exploit to produce food, housing, and other material needs. Thus the terrain, the lack of potential converts and labor, the absence of precious metals, and a forbidding climate combined to keep the line of Spanish settlement far to the south of Oklahoma. Later, when the Plains Indians secured horses, an even more formidable barrier insulated Oklahoma from Spanish influence.

The *entradas* of Coronado, De Soto, Oñate, and others did provide the basis for Spain's claim to the major portion of North America. For over three hundred years all or portions of modern Oklahoma were in territory held first by Spain and then by independent Mexico. In the seventeenth century both France and England challenged Spain for control of the continent. After La Salle explored the Mississippi in 1682, France laid claim to a vast inland empire which included Oklahoma. During the Seven Years' War, Spain, France, and England all sought to possess the region that included what is now Oklahoma. The treaties that ended the war in 1763 awarded the area to Spain as part of the Louisiana Territory. In 1800, however, Napoleon forced the decadent Spanish government to cede Louisiana to France but promised that if he did not want to keep it, he would return the land to Spain. Three years later, however, Napoleon suddenly sold Louisiana to the United States. The exact boundaries of the newly acquired territory were indefinite until the United States and Spain negotiated the Adams-Onís Treaty in 1819, when all but the modern Oklahoma Panhandle passed under American control. Territory beyond the 100th meridian remained in Spanish hands until Mexico gained independence in 1821. From 1821 to 1836, the Oklahoma Panhandle was part of the Mexican province of Texas and remained a Mexican possession until Texas revolted against Mexican rule in 1836. Between 1836 and 1848, Mexico refused to recognize first the independence of Texas and then its annexation to the United States. The Oklahoma Panhandle, therefore, was still considered part of the Republic of Mexico. Finally, in the Treaty of Guadalupe Hidalgo (1848), Mexico ceded over one-half of its national territory to the United States after the Mexican War. The cession included Texas, and therefore the last portion of modern Oklahoma "officially" passed from Mexican possession.

For almost two hundred years, numerous trails and roads stretching through Oklahoma provided commercial contact with colonial and independent Mexico. In the eighteenth century, the Spanish opened the Old Spanish Road to the Red River, which they called El Río Nutrio. This road began at Santa Fe, crossed the Texas Panhandle, entered Oklahoma at the 100th meridian near the north fork of the Red River, crossed that branch twice, and followed the main stream to a terminus on the Washita. In the nineteenth century, one branch of the famous Santa Fe Trail, which extended from the great bend of the Missouri to New Mexico, sliced across the Oklahoma Panhandle. In 1839 Josiah Gregg crossed Oklahoma en route to Santa Fe and Chihuahua. He returned the following year with twenty-eight cargo-laden wagons and several hundred sheep, goats, and mules. The Texas Road, which also passed through Oklahoma, became the most important artery between American settlements in Missouri and Kansas and the Mexican province of Texas. Thus, before the present Southwest was incorporated into the United States in 1848, Oklahoma served as an important avenue for men and goods going to and coming from Mexican territory.

After the Civil War, the great cattle trails funneled millions of

Mexican longhorns from Texas through Oklahoma to railheads in Missouri and Kansas. These drives followed the East and West Shawnee trails, the Chisholm Trail, and the Great Western Trail. Thousands of cowboys, many of them Mexicans or *tejanos* (Texans of Mexican descent), symbolized the Spanish-Mexican influence on the culture of the American Southwest. The American cowboy directly borrowed the practices, equipment, and much of the vocabulary of the Spanish-Mexican ranching culture. Spaniards and Mexicans were the first to establish ranches *(ranchos)* and tend cattle on horseback in North America. They introduced the practice of branding, which dated from the Moorish occupation of Spain during the Middle Ages. Their clothing and equipment included chaps *(chaparejos)*, a lariat or lasso *(la reata* or *lazo),* and the wide-brimmed sombrero.

Along the cattle trail, a buckaroo *(vaquero)* traveled through patches of chaparral *(chaparro)* and mesquite (Spanish *"mezquite"* from Aztec *"mizquitl").* Lobos and coyotes (Spanish *"coyote"* from Aztec *"coyotl"*) attacked his cattle or the *remuda* (the string of extra horses). He often had to cross *arroyos* or circle canyons *(cañones)* and mesas. For fun, the cowboy participated in an impromptu or formal rodeo and risked his personal safety trying to ride a mustang *(mesteño)* or a bronco. After celebrating too much in a trail town, he was taken to the hoosegow *(juzgado)* and thrown into the calaboose *(calabozo).* Words such as "fiesta," "compadre," "amigo," and "vamoose" *(vámonos)* peppered his vocabulary. The Spanish-Mexican culture played an important role in the everyday life of the Oklahoma cowboy.

Spanish-Mexican influence revolutionized the life and culture of the Southern Plains Indian. Before the arrival of the Spaniards, the Indian had no animal he could ride and none save the travois-pulling dog whose power he could harness. Once the Indian captured and learned to ride the Spanish horse, his life changed dramatically. By the early 1700s the Apache, Comanche, or Kiowa warrior was an expert rider. The Indian hunter could move as fast as the buffalo and kill him with a well-placed arrow. He struck his enemy with terrifying swiftness and quickly retreated to safety. The Indian's mobility, possessions, and wealth (usually measured by the number of horses he owned) increased significantly.

After acquiring the horse, the Indian was the most formidable obstacle to Spanish penetration of the plains. For almost two hundred years—until the end of the Southern Plains War—the Apaches, Kiowas, and Comanches raided hundreds of miles into Mexico. The

Comanches were some of the finest light cavalry in history. During the raids into Mexico it was customary to take captives, especially young boys, who were carried north of the border and ransomed, sold, or incorporated into the tribe. In the 1860s and 1870s, the tribes intensified their raids in a desperate attempt to bolster their dwindling ranks. Witnesses reported that Indians were taking young Mexican boys from settlements all across the northern tier of states. Many of these captives became famous in battle or in tribal councils. These young men were the first permanent, albeit involuntary, Mexican immigrants to Oklahoma.[1]

While the Plains Indians raided into Mexico, other Oklahoma tribes viewed that country as a potential place of settlement, where they could maintain or return to their old way of life, untainted or unencumbered by the white man. In the mid-1830s, John Ross of the Cherokees considered purchasing land in Mexico as an alternative to forced removal to Oklahoma. Later, in 1845, Ross and a party of fifty-four Cherokees visited Mexican territory to examine the possibility of establishing a settlement there. In 1849 the Seminole leader Wild Cat led a group of his people and some Negroes into Mexico and established a small community across from Eagle Pass, Texas.

Other groups of Indians periodically investigated the possibility of moving to Mexico after this time, but few left Oklahoma. Renewed interest in Mexican colonization arose after the passage of the Dawes Act (1887) and the Curtis Act (1898), which imposed land allotments on the Five Civilized Tribes, divided their property, and dissolved their governments. In 1896 Jacob B. Jackson, an elderly Choctaw fullblood, became the leader of a Mexican emigration plan which ultimately included other tribes and for a time assumed an official character. In 1906 he asked a visiting United States Senate committee to allow his followers to sell their allotments and purchase land for a colony in Mexico. The committee ridiculed his idea, and the national administration ignored it.

The Kickapoos had a closer relationship with Mexico than any other Oklahoma Indian tribe. They entered Texas while it was still a province of Mexico and lived peacefully there during its first years as a republic. In 1839, when Mirabeau B. Lamar drove many of the Indians out of Texas, most of the Kickapoos fled into Oklahoma; about eighty, however, crossed the Río Grande into Mexico. During the Civil War, a portion of the Kickapoos moved to Kansas, while about twelve hundred others joined their relatives in Mexico. They settled near Nacimiento, Coahuila, where the Mexicans welcomed

Michael M. Smith

Lawrie Tatum, agent of the Kiowa Agency, and five Mexican boys who had been captured by the Comanches. Courtesy of the Oklahoma Historical Society.

them as a protective barrier against Kiowa and Comanche raids.

In 1865 the Kickapoos in Kansas reluctantly settled on a reservation in Oklahoma. Most soon abandoned their lands, however, and about 150 went to Mexico. When they returned to Oklahoma two years later, only about five square miles of their lands remained. Meanwhile, the Kickapoos in Mexico had settled down to farming and hunting and supplemented their income by raiding across the Río Grande into Texas. After Texas appealed to the United States government for help in 1873, Colonel Ranald S. McKenzie raided the camp and forced over three hundred Kickapoos to return to Oklahoma. During the next two years, about 150 more joined their tribe on a reservation between the North Canadian and the Deep Fork. Another 350 remained in Nacimiento.

Forced allotment ultimately led to the systematic despoliation of the Kickapoo lands in Oklahoma. After 1900 hundreds migrated to Mexico, settling at Músquiz, near Nacimiento, and at Bacerac, a barren, rocky area in Sonora across from Douglas, Arizona. Even in Mexico, predatory whites conspired with local Mexican officials

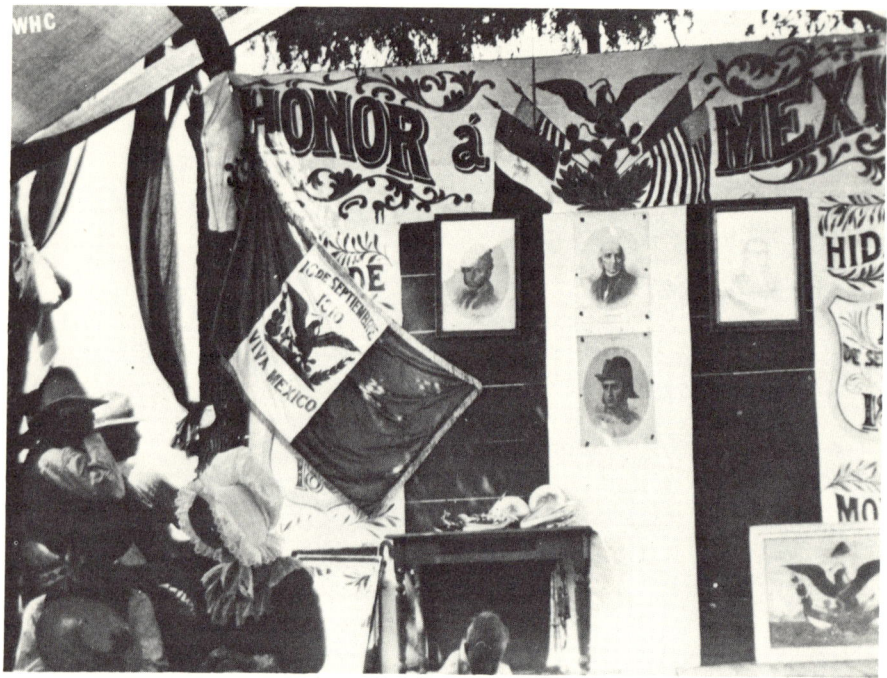

Display at the Mexican Independence Day celebration at Anadarko, September 16, 1901. Father Hidalgo, who started the revolt against Spain, is in the center top photograph. Courtesy of the Western History Collections, University of Oklahoma.

to force the Kickapoos to cede their allotments. Some of the Kickapoos in Mexico later returned to what was left of their land in Oklahoma. Hundreds of others continued to reside in Mexico. Even today, they periodically move from one settlement to the other.[2]

Only a few accounts mentioned Mexicans living in Oklahoma prior to 1900. Although many romantic legends related that Mexicans had discovered and mined rich gold deposits throughout the southwestern part of the state, there was scant evidence to support such contentions. Occasionally someone reported that a band of "Mexican" desperados was hiding out at one place or another. A particular retreat was a place called "Mexican Rendezvous," located on the Washita River southeast of Pauls Valley. An early settler noted that there was a Mexican settlement near Anadarko. Every September the residents held a picnic during which Mexicans and Indians matched their skills in roping and riding. In 1899 the *El Reno News*

Display at the Mexican Independence Day celebration at Anadarko, September 16, 1901. Courtesy of the Western History Collections, University of Oklahoma.

reported that about three hundred Mexicans dedicated to raising sheep were living in Beaver County near the New Mexico line. By the turn of the century, increasing numbers of Mexicans were working on railroad construction gangs, in the coal mines of the old Choctaw Nation, in the cotton fields, and on farms and ranches throughout Oklahoma. The major migration of Mexicans to Oklahoma, however, did not begin until after statehood. Thousands of Mexican immigrants would be both attracted by the increasing opportunities for employment in the state's expanding economy and pushed by the progressively deteriorating conditions prevailing in their native land.[3]

Chapter 2

HISTORICAL ANTECEDENTS TO MEXICAN MIGRATION

The increasing presence of Mexicans in Oklahoma at the beginning of the twentieth century reflected the poverty, oppression, and dislocation which the masses of that country had endured for generations. Mostly poor *campesinos* (peasants), they responded to conditions in Mexico by the only means left to them—voluntary migration. They were the victims of a combination of historical circumstances that dated as far back as the Spanish conquest and over which they had little or no control.

On August 13, 1521, as Hernán Cortés and his soldiers stalked the still-smoldering ruins of the Aztec capital, México-Tenochtitlán, the most powerful indigenous civilization in Mexico was ended. Within a relatively short time, the Spaniards conquered almost all sedentary cultures in central Mexico and established new institutions to replace the formal organization of Indian society. Inspired by priests to eradicate all vestiges of the Indians' pagan religion, soldiers destroyed temples and pyramids and eliminated the indigenous elite. To reward the conquerors, Spain granted them *encomiendas,* semifeudal institutions by which the Spaniards received tribute and labor from a particular group of natives. The *encomienda* did not give a Spaniard title to Indian lands, and the natives continued to live in their villages and till their communal fields.

To fulfill its obligation to convert, Christianize, and civilize the Indians, the Spanish crown relied upon the Roman Catholic Church. In many respects, however, the Church succeeded only in providing a thin veneer of Catholicism over deeply ingrained and conservative Indian religions. A good example of the syncretic nature of the resultant religion was the Virgin of Guadalupe. The Aztecs had revered the goddess Tonantzin ("Our Mother") and made pilgrimages to her temple located just north of Mexico City. In 1531, according to tradition, the Virgin Mary appeared on three different occasions near the same site to a young Indian named Juan Diego. The Virgin's appearance had a tremendous effect on the Indians and greatly facilitated their conversion to Christianity. The Virgin of Guadalupe, whose dark features are unmistakably Indian, became the focal point of Mexican Catholicism and the patron saint of the nation. Her feast day, observed on December 12, became the most important religious celebration in Mexico.

In the decades after the conquest the Spanish elite continued to arrogate political and economic power, while the Indians slipped farther to the margins of society. Meanwhile, the indigenous cultures suffered a demographic disaster. Partly as a result of overwork and mistreatment, but principally because of widespread epidemics of European diseases, by about 1650 the native population declined by nearly 85 percent. By the end of the seventeenth century, vast amounts of land were unoccupied. These factors led to the growth of large privately owned estates called *haciendas*. To assure themselves a steady work supply, the *hacendados* (landowners) encouraged Indians and *mestizos* (Spanish-Indian mixed bloods) to accumulate a debt at the *tienda de raya* (the hacienda's commissary store) or through loans for personal emergencies, fiestas, or church fees. Although he was not a slave, the *peón* was not free to leave the *hacienda* until his debt to the *patrón* was paid. This system of debt bondage—peonage—enabled the *hacendados* to exercise the prerogatives of a quasi-feudal aristocracy.

Social status in colonial Mexico was based on race or ethnicity. The principal social classes were comprised of the whites (European-born *peninsulares* and Mexican-born *criollos*), *mestizos,* and Indians. The *peninsulares* monopolized the most important civil and religious positions. *Criollos,* who came to possess much of the land and mineral wealth, were generally regarded by the *peninsulares* as inferiors, tainted by their place of birth. The *mestizos,* considered outcasts by both whites and Indians, were forced to seek their own small plots of land, join the urban proletariat, or succumb to peonage. The white elite either completely ignored the Indian majority or unconscionably exploited them.

This inflexible system helped provoke the movement for independence which began on September 16, 1810, under the leadership of Father Miguel Hidalgo y Costilla, and terminated in 1821 when the forces of Augustín de Iturbide defeated the last Spanish army. Independence eliminated the *peninsulares,* but the new *criollo* elite and the powerful Church did not encourage significant alteration of the basic structure of Mexican society. Indians and *mestizos* remained largely on the margins of national life. An entrenched conservative triarchy, composed of the *hacendados,* the church, and the army, successfully resisted any challenge to their privileged position in the new state.

The first fifty-five years of Mexican independence were marred by bitter civil wars between liberals, who wanted to create a federalized, secular, bourgeois republic, and conservatives, who preferred a centralized, aristocratic government that would protect their privileges. Mexico suffered invasions by foreign powers and experienced the humiliating loss of over one-half of her national domain in a war with the United States. Throughout the period the *criollo* elite proved only that they were incapable of governing the country. In 1854 a resurgent liberal party, comprised principally of *mestizos* and Indians and led by Benito Juárez, a fullblood Zapotec Indian, sought to destroy the old order and create a middle-class agrarian democracy in Mexico. The attempted reforms provoked a three-year bloodbath known as the War of the Reform (1857–1860). During the conflict, the liberals' major target was the Catholic Church, which employed its vast financial resources to support the conservatives. The liberals nationalized church properties and attacked its monopoly of education, civil records, cemeteries, and marriage.

Although they emerged victorious in 1860, the liberals merely sowed the seeds of further strife. Alienated conservatives sought to establish a monarchy headed by a European prince who would restore order and their privileges. Abysmal political and economic conditions encouraged foreign meddling in Mexican affairs. In 1862, using Mexico's unpaid debts to French creditors as an excuse, Napoleon III of France ordered an invasion of Mexico. Although the Mexican liberals, under the command of General Ignacio Zaragosa, successfully defended Puebla on May 5, 1862, the French army and thousands of Mexican conservatives finally drove Juárez from the country. Two years later, with French financial and military support, Archduke Maximilian of Austria was crowned emperor of Mexico. Maximilian's ill-fated empire lasted only three years. In 1867, after another devastating civil war, he was captured and executed. Juárez once again assumed the presidency.

After over one-half century of civil strife, Mexico needed a strong hand and a long period of uninterrupted stability to further her economic development. The great mass of Mexicans lived in poverty and ignorance. Ninety percent of the Mexican people were illiterate. Petty *caudillos* (strong men) dominated state and local governments. The country had made almost no progress towards industrialization; the mines were closed, and agricultural production languished. Mexico could not even pay the interest on her foreign debts. Few city streets were safe, and bandits plagued the highways and countryside. Unless someone could restore order, protect lives and property, and develop Mexico's transportation and industrial systems, the country would continue to stagnate.

In 1876 General Porfirio Díaz, supported by the army, seized power. Díaz controlled Mexico for the next thirty-five years and oversaw a period of unprecedented peace and economic advancement. By 1910 the value of Mexican imports and exports had risen over one thousand percent. Mexico became a world leader in the production of gold, silver, and petroleum. Encouraged by stability and Díaz's liberal concessions, foreigners invested over two billion dollars in the country. Díaz promised businessmen a cheap, docile labor supply and no problems of unionization or governmental interference. Foreigners soon gained control of Mexican mines and oil reserves, textile mills and retail outlets, public utilities, railroads, and vast stretches of land. Many Mexicans lamented that during the *Porfiriato,* Mexico became the "mother of foreigners and the stepmother of Mexicans."

The peace and prosperity of the Porfirian period, however, was only a cruel facade. Foreigners and a favored few Mexicans reaped the benefits of Don Porfirio's rule, while the Mexican masses were submerged in poverty and despair. Land concentration accelerated during the Díaz era as thousands of Indian villages were absorbed by land companies, politicos, and neighboring *haciendas.* Although over 80 percent of the population was employed in some aspect of agriculture, 95 percent of the land was owned by five thousand families. *Hacendados* numbered their holdings in the tens or hundreds of thousands of acres; the politically powerful Terrazas family of Chihuahua owned estates totaling nearly 6.6 million square acres.

A rapid rise in population during the *Porfiriato*—from about nine million in 1876 to nearly fifteen million in 1910—combined with the shrinking amount of available land to intensify Mexico's agrarian problems. Over one-third of the total population was trapped in debt peonage, in reality nothing more than legalized slavery. A family's debt passed from generation to generation, and peons were often bought with the land or traded and sold as chattel. The Mexican peasant—bound *peón* or free *campesino*—lived in ignorance and abject poverty—virtually a condition of semi-starvation. Over 80 percent of the rural population was illiterate. A typical *peón* family lived, ate, and slept in a windowless, one-room adobe shack with a dirt floor. Large families shared their cramped quarters with chickens or other animals they might be fortunate enough to possess. Their diet consisted largely of corn (from which they made the all-purpose *tortillas*), beans, *chile*, and rice, often supplemented by generous quantities of *pulque*, a nutritious but mildly intoxicating beverage made from the juice of maguey plant. Filthy and unsanitary living conditions spawned numerous endemic diseases. Over 30 percent of all infants died in their first year.

Static wages and rising costs exacerbated the plight of the Mexican masses. The average daily wage for farm labor never rose above twenty-five cents in American currency between 1880 and 1910, while the cost of everyday needs rose over 100 percent in the same period. With minor exceptions, workers in areas of highest demographic concentration—principally the central plateau region—received the lowest pay. Mining occupations and other types of work reflected a similar ratio.[1]

The system allowed the masses no effective means to redress their grievances or improve their lot. The *peón*'s only recourse was flight—if he could elude the *Guardias Rurales*, Díaz's rural militia. In the first decade of the twentieth century, textile workers in Puebla and Veracruz and miners in Sonora attempted to strike for higher wages and better working conditions. State militias and federal troops mercilessly massacred hundreds of them.

In September 1910, Díaz invited thousands of foreign guests to Mexico City to attend the celebration commemorating the nation's first one hundred years of independence and his own eightieth birthday. All were duly impressed by the peace and prosperity they observed in the beautiful capital. What they saw, however, was only illusory. Desperate peasants were ready to strike back at those who had stolen their lands. Young intellectuals were alienated from a system which stifled their careers in government and gave preference to foreigners. Laborers in the mines, in the factories, and on the railroads, who worked under dangerous conditions for low wages, were seething for change. In less than two months after the centennial celebration, the old order began to crumble. A revolution—The Mexican Revolution—the first great social upheaval of the twentieth century, would wipe away the old regime and inundate Mexico with violence for the next decade.

The revolution erupted in 1910 under the nominal leadership of Francisco I. Madero, an *hacendado* from Coahuila, whose own political and economic interests had suffered under Díaz. Madero was joined by Emiliano Zapata, an Indian from Morelos who simply sought to return village lands to the men who tilled them. Francisco "Pancho" Villa, an ex-bandit from Durango, gained a large and dedicated following among the *campesinos* in the north. Venustiano Carranza, former senator and governor of Coahuila and a reluctant revolutionary, would ultimately emerge as the dominant force of the revolution. He was aided by numerous military chieftains, the most important of whom was Alvaro Obregón of Sonora.

The revolutionaries sought to end dictatorship, regain control of Mexico's economy and natural resources, redistribute the land and wealth, provide protection and adequate wages for workers, and establish a decent standard of living and education for the Mexican people. The revolution uprooted thousands of peasant families as leaders abolished peonage, broke up many of the *haciendas,* and destroyed the traditional bonds between *patrón* and *peón.* Thousands joined the revolutionary bands, often taking their women and children with them. Thousands more simply fled in fright. The violence caused devastation of fields and villages, loss of employment, food shortages, famines, and epidemics. Although the revolution was not the primary cause of the exodus of thousands of Mexicans to the United States, it was a catalyst for a process already underway.[2]

Chapter 3
MIGRATION AND SETTLEMENT IN OKLAHOMA

A variety of factors coalesced during the first three decades of the twentieth century to cause massive immigration of Mexicans into the United States. For almost two generations before the revolution, Mexican laborers had developed pronounced internal migratory tendencies as a result of demographic pressures, low wages, the expansion of mining and ranching in the north, and the extension of railroad lines to the border of the United States. In addition, between 1900 and 1930 the American Southwest experienced rapid economic growth as large-scale agriculture, mining, and railroad activities attracted millions of dollars of investment and created increasing demands for labor. The period also marked the growing restriction of immigration to the United States and the consequent elimination of a ready supply of cheap labor from Europe and the Orient. This caused American agriculturalists and businessmen to develop an increasing dependence upon Mexico as a source of workers.

Inhabitants of the central plateau most sharply felt the effects of economic problems during the *Porfiriato.* This area, including the states of Jalisco, Michoacán, and Guanajuato, was the most fertile and heavily populated portion of Mexico. Here, a few *hacendados* held most of the land, and a labor surplus depressed agricultural wages. The central plateau contained the oldest and most important gold and silver deposits, but miners fared little better than *campesinos.* Their relatively low wages before the revolution were reduced even further by dependence upon the *tienda de raya,* which sold goods at inflated prices. The same conditions existed to a lesser extent in the states of Aguascalientes, Zacatecas, San Luis Potosí, and Durango.[1]

By the 1890s thousands of peasants from the central plateau

roamed over Mexico in search of jobs. Many drifted into the growing cities of Monterrey, Guadalajara, San Luis Potosí, and Mexico City and joined the burgeoning urban proletariat. Others moved north into the less densely populated states of Sonora, Chihuahua, Coahuila, Tamaulipas, and Nuevo León, where the development of mining, railroads, and ranching had led to a demand for labor and generally higher wages. Because of the shortage of labor in the north, mine operators actively recruited and imported workers from the old mining centers of Guanajuato, Zacatecas, and San Luis Potosí. As early as 1900, *hacendados* in the central plateau complained that they were suffering a labor shortage.

In addition to the *campesinos* and miners of the central plateau, other types of migratory labor were common before the revolution. Small, semi-tribal groups of people living in clusters of primitive huts called *rancherías* wandered throughout the country in search of employment. They lived in squatters' camps near mines, railway junctions, *haciendas,* and cities where they might find seasonal jobs. *Criollos* or *mestizos* who valued private property often became temporary migrants to earn money which would enable them to buy a piece of land near their home village. As early as 1870 they worked on south Texas ranches or sharecropped in the irrigated agricultural regions. While some remained in Texas, most returned to Nuevo León, Tamaulipas, and Coahuila to purchase their own small properties. Thus, even before large numbers of *campesinos* migrated to the United States during and after the revolution, substantial internal movement was already under way in Mexico.[2]

The growing supply of available Mexican labor occurred simultaneously with the economic development of the American Southwest. Work in the cotton fields, citrus groves, mining camps, beet fields, and on the railroads attracted Mexicans to Texas, Arizona, New Mexico, Colorado, California, Oklahoma, Kansas, and Nebraska. All of these industries required large amounts of unskilled labor. Since the Southwest was an area of sparse population, the labor shortage also created relatively high wages. Unskilled railroad workers could earn as much as $1.25 in gold a day in Texas, $1.75 in California, and even more in the states beyond the Mexican-American border. In agricultural work, a field hand could earn from fifty cents to two dollars a day, while mining paid almost $2.50 a day for common labor. The economic expansion of the Southwest occurred at a time when native American workers' wages and standard of living were rising rapidly. Few Americans were willing to perform the backbreaking labor that was demanded in the Southwest when they could find more attractive and more remunerative employment elsewhere. While most native workers refused to migrate to the Southwest, foreign sources of labor increasingly diminished during the period. The Chinese Exclusion Act (1882) and the "Gentleman's Agreement" with Japan (1907) effectively excluded Oriental "coolie" labor. By 1917 the United States immigration requirements excluded such persons as known criminals, mental or physical defectives, paupers or those likely to become public charges, alien contract laborers, and illiterate adults. Despite these restrictions, however, immigration from southern and eastern Europe continued during the first two decades of the twentieth century. Americans whose ancestors had come principally from northern and western Europe began to fear that the ethnic background, customs, language, and religions of the "new immigrants" were weakening the very foundations of the "American way of life." In addition, organized labor decried their willingness to work for low wages and serve as scabs or strikebreakers. In 1921 and 1924, new immigration acts assigned each nation a quota based on the resident population of the United States and reduced the total number of immigrants allowed under that quota system to 150,000 annually. As a result, the Southwest increasingly depended upon Mexican labor.[3]

While the problems of unemployment, static wages, land concentration, and peonage provided the major impetus to Mexican migration after 1900, the construction of railroad lines across the northern desert of Mexico allowed the jobless *campesino* to reach the burgeoning labor market and high wages beyond the Río Grande. Between 1882 and 1912, four major railroad companies constructed lines stretching thousands of miles from the United States border to the Mexican heartland. The Mexican International reached Eagle Pass in 1882. The Mexican National completed a connection to Laredo that same year and in 1904 extended a line to Brownsville. In 1884 the Mexican Central linked Mexico City with El Paso. By 1912 the extensive Mexican portion of the Southern Pacific swept up the western side of Mexico to California and New Mexico.

Railroad construction bosses recruited their laborers from the agricultural population along the lines. At first the *campesino* signed on for a short time, usually for a period of days or a few weeks between crops. But as construction reached farther north, he remained for longer periods. Initially the *campesino* was reluctant to work or sleep away from home. Gradually, however, as he became more attached to cash wages, he signed on for a month or more to work hundreds of miles up and down the line. He became accustomed to having silver in his pocket and bought things he had never dreamed of owning. The *campesino* finally lost his reluctance to leave his village and settled more readily in the railway towns.

The northern portions of the railroads passed through sparsely inhabited regions where resident labor was in short supply. Railroad companies employed workers from the central regions as construction workers or section hands and gave them free transportation home when their job was finished. Gradually, therefore, the central Mexican villager moved to within a few miles of the border. Thousands of railroad workers refused to take their free transportation home and crossed into the United States, where eager American employers welcomed them with a gold wage. Miners also migrated to the United States. Mine operators found it increasingly difficult to hold labor. In 1908 one mining official claimed that 80 percent of his labor force had deserted to work in Arizona and New Mexico.

As word of the exciting opportunities in the United States radiated throughout the interior of Mexico, thousands of *campesinos* sold their animals or borrowed money from family or friends to purchase a railway ticket to the border. Peasants, often with their families, walked twenty-five or fifty miles to railway stations in Jalisco and Guanajuato, where passage to El Paso cost from twenty to twenty-five pesos. Many *campesinos* who could not afford a ticket walked great distances to the border. A penniless migrant and his family often traveled as much as three hundred miles on foot to reach the frontier.

During the first decade of the twentieth century, Mexican labor inexorably moved from the central plateau to the northern Mexican states and finally into the border states and territories of the United States. After the revolution began, thousands more followed essentially the same path. The vast majority of these migrants were poverty-stricken Indians and *mestizos,* but people of all races and economic classes left Mexico to seek the economic opportunities which the United States offered.

The *campesinos* typically came to the United States expecting to work a short time and then return to Mexico. Most migrants were males, either single or married men traveling alone, who came north in search of seasonal employment. Every payday thousands of Mexican workers sent money orders to their families back home. Recognizing the cyclical nature of migration, railroad companies gave their

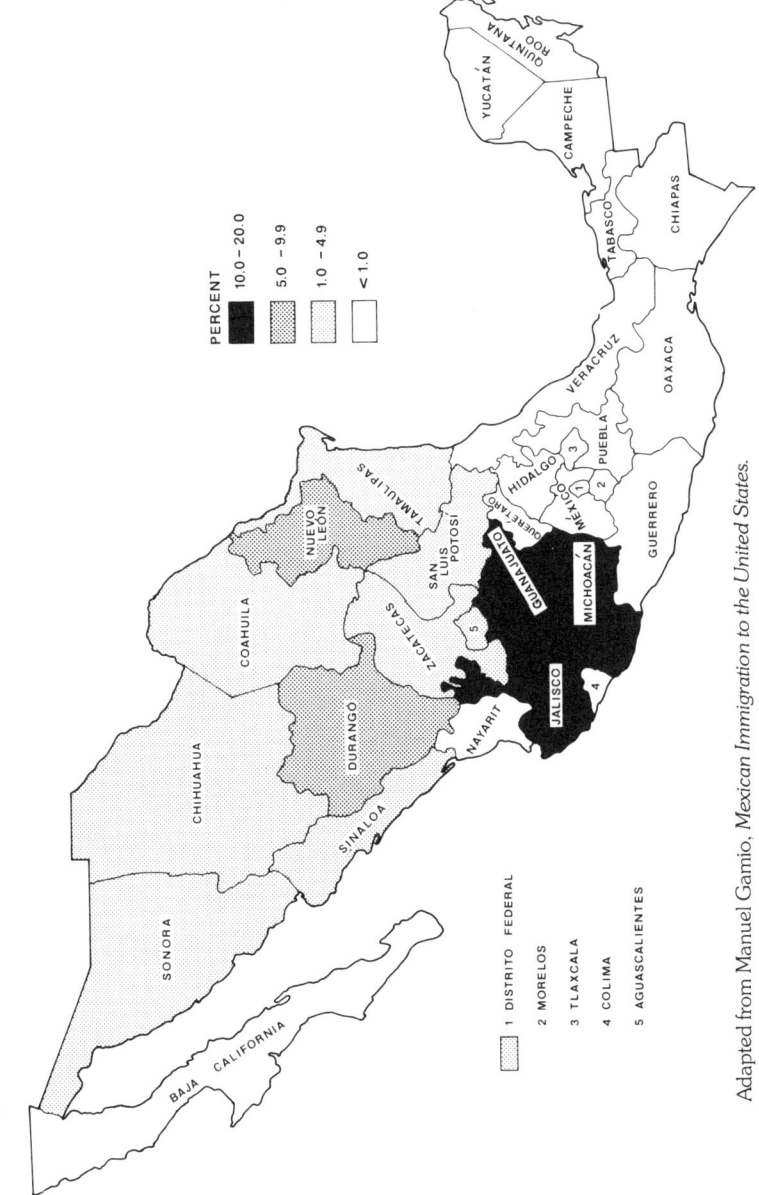

SOURCES OF MEXICAN IMMIGRATION TO THE UNITED STATES IN 1926
BASED ON TOTAL PERCENT OF MONEY ORDERS RECEIVED BY STATE OR TERRITORY

PERCENT

10.0 – 20.0

5.0 – 9.9

1.0 – 4.9

< 1.0

1 DISTRITO FEDERAL
2 MORELOS
3 TLAXCALA
4 COLIMA
5 AGUASCALIENTES

Adapted from Manuel Gamio, *Mexican Immigration to the United States.*

Mexican employees passes to return free of charge or at reduced rates to the border town where they had been recruited. After the revolution, migratory patterns changed considerably. The social, economic, and political dislocation forced many Mexicans to remain longer in the United States while they waited for the situation to stabilize.[4]

As the immigrant reached one of the American border towns, agents obligingly facilitated his contact with a variety of employers. American companies sent their recruiters to the border or used private agencies which engaged exclusively in securing Mexican workers. El Paso was the principal center of recruiting activity. Here agencies advanced the Mexican peasant board, lodging, and transportation to a place of employment. The railroads were the single most important employer of Mexican labor. They relied principally upon two types of agencies. Some operators shipped Mexicans for a fee, which the railroad rather than the individual immigrant usually paid. The other principal type of supplier was the commissary company, which recruited men for the railroads as a secondary line of business. These companies were interested in keeping extra railroad gangs up to full strength in order to maximize their profits from the sale of commissary goods to railroad crews. While some companies did not charge fees for their services, others did so when the labor market allowed them the opportunity. At its El Paso offices, one commissary company maintained a labor bureau dedicated exclusively to supplying Mexican track workers for the Santa Fe.

The increased demand for labor during and immediately after World War I encouraged a large number of independent agents to operate in the border towns. These labor contractors, whom the Mexicans called *enganchistas* ("hookers"), offered Mexicans contracts as soon as they crossed the border. Often disregarding the contract labor law, *enganchistas* entered Mexico to advertise the many opportunities and high wages available in the United States.

El Paso, which had direct rail contact with the central plateau and was located near the mobile mining population of Chihuahua, became the major distribution center for Mexican labor in the United States. Three major railroads had a terminus in that city and drew heavily on Mexicans as a source of cheap, unskilled labor. The railways then became the major feeders for other industries throughout the Southwest and elsewhere. West of El Paso, Mexicans crossed the border to seek employment in the mining fields of New Mexico, Arizona, California, and Colorado. East of El Paso, the major crossing points were Eagle Pass, Laredo, and Brownsville, from which points laborers found employment on railroads, ranches, and farms. El Paso was the only border city that served as a true labor depot. Other major distribution centers from which Mexicans spread throughout the country included San Antonio, Kansas City, Los Angeles, Tucson, and Trinidad and Denver, Colorado.[5]

Before 1900 Mexican immigration went largely unnoticed, but by 1908 the increasing volume merited serious attention. Not until 1917, however, did American authorities apply the literacy test or the head tax to Mexicans. Mexicans faced few restrictions upon entry and were not required to have passports before 1918. One long-time Oklahoma resident, who came to the United States in 1914, stated that all he had to do to enter the country was pay a nickel to cross the bridge at El Paso. No one asked him anything, and he did not volunteer any information. Most Mexicans who reached the border were penniless and would have been denied entry at an eastern port; nevertheless, they were admitted without question. During the violent phase of the revolution, as thousands of refugees fled across the border, most immigration officials quietly ignored the restrictions. These people, they believed, would return to their homes as soon as the violence ended.

After the outbreak of World War I, American authorities lowered the border restrictions even further. The war drastically reduced the number of immigrants from across the Atlantic, and millions of Americans served in the armed forces or found better paying jobs in war-related industries. American employers sought and received permission to employ Mexican contract laborers, who were exempt from the literacy test and the eight-dollar head tax. Between 1917 and 1921, 72,862 Mexicans legally entered the United States as temporary laborers. By June 1921, over 21,000 had deserted their employment and remained illegally in the country. This high incidence of unlawful immigration continued until the Great Depression. Between 1911 and 1930, the heaviest period of Mexican immigration, the United States legally admitted over 678,000 immigrants. An uncertain number of others entered without documents during that time. Thousands of Mexicans and their families who could not meet the requirements of health, literacy, head tax, visa fee, or self-support crossed the border without inspection. These illegal entrants were called *mojados* ("wetbacks"), presumably because they swam across the Río Grande to avoid border officials. In later years the term was applied to any Mexican residing illegally in the United States. Although undocumented aliens constantly ran the risk of deportation, thousands crossed undeterred.[6]

Given the poverty, timidity, and general inexperience of the *campesino*, other forces were required to encourage his illegal entry into a strange land and an often prejudiced and hostile environment. Most *mojados* relied upon *"coyotes"* (smugglers) who plied the border and interior towns of Mexico. The *"coyotes"* knew the routes past immigration officials, rented "safe houses" in border towns, and maintained contact with *enganchistas* on the American side. For a price—collected both from the migrant and the *enganchista*—the *"coyote"* would steer the *mojado* across the border. From Texas to California, the *"coyotes,"* the *enganchistas*, and the recruiting agents of American employers continually fed migrants into the labor market.

In 1940 a United States congressional hearing held in Oklahoma City revealed that illegal recruiting practices had persisted into the early 1930s. One witness related that just across the Río Grande, *enganchistas* established offices and collected from fifty cents to one dollar for each worker they supplied to a railroad, ranch, or other business. An official of the Texas State Employment Service testified that when the labor supply was short, *"coyotes"* regularly received a fee for each worker they delivered; when the market was plentiful, American enterprises retained *"coyotes"* on salary.[7]

By 1930 the total recorded Mexican-born population in the United States was 639,017. The states with large Mexican-born populations included Texas (262,672), California (191,346), Arizona (47,855), Illinois (20,069), and Kansas (11,012). Oklahoma counted 3,496 residents born in Mexico. Mexicans had established *colonias* (colonies) or *barrios* (ghettos) in all large southwestern cities and in the major midwestern and northern industrial centers including Kansas City, St. Louis, Chicago, Detroit, and Pittsburgh. Including *mojados*, the Mexican-born population was nearly 1.5 million. This massive wave of immigration slowed to a mere trickle with the onset of the depression. Figures on Mexican immigration were highly unreliable, but between 1901 and 1930 about 728,000 Mexicans legally entered the United States. From 1931 to 1940, however, only 23,000 were formally admitted. Competition for the few jobs available and hostility to alien workers provided an unfriendly climate for Mexicans. Between 1931 and 1940, about 450,000 (including women and children) "repatriated"—most of them under pressure—to their native land.

In 1940 the United States census indicated that the Mexican-born population was 377,433 as opposed to 639,017 in 1930. In addition, it noted that the Mexican-descent population included 619,300 second-generation persons of foreign or mixed parentage and 628,000 of native parentage. Because many Mexicans feared deportation during the depression years, a large number avoided the census taker. In 1940 there were approximately 2,125,000 persons of Mexican descent residing in the United States.[8]

The precise number and distribution of Mexicans in Oklahoma during the period from 1900 to 1940 was uncertain. The data for this period included only those Mexicans who were counted at a particular place on a specific date at ten-year intervals. Since most Mexicans were highly mobile, often lived in isolated rural camps where census takers seldom ventured, or were illegal residents who avoided enumeration, more doubtless resided in Oklahoma than the figures indicated.

The immigration and distribution patterns for Mexicans in Oklahoma generally reflected national trends between 1900 and 1940. In 1900 there were only 134 Mexicans officially recorded for Oklahoma, sixty-four in Indian Territory and seventy in Oklahoma Territory. Of the Indian Territory residents, thirty-one lived in the Chickasaw Nation and twenty-three in the Choctaw Nation. Undoubtedly, these immigrants were employed principally in the coal mines of that region.[9]

As Oklahoma's economy developed after statehood, the Mexican population rose dramatically. In 1910, the national census recorded 2,645 Mexican-born residents in the state. They worked principally in the coal mines, on railroad section gangs, and in the agricultural and ranching areas. Oklahoma County recorded the largest number of Mexican immigrants with a total of 449. Of these, 379 lived in Oklahoma City, where most worked for the Santa Fe, Frisco, Rock Island, and Katy railroads. Other counties showing a significant population included Kay (378), Logan (238), Jefferson (211), Comanche (109), and Lincoln (103).[10]

By 1920 the Mexican-born population had risen to 6,697, an increase of more than 250 percent over 1910. Mexicans were employed not only in railroads, mines, agriculture, and ranching, but also in packinghouses, oil fields, quarries, and numerous unskilled positions in industry and municipal services. Cities with the largest Mexican populations included Oklahoma City (788), Tulsa (168), and Bartlesville (122). Counties recording the highest number of Mexicans included Oklahoma (821), Kay (471), Comanche (417),

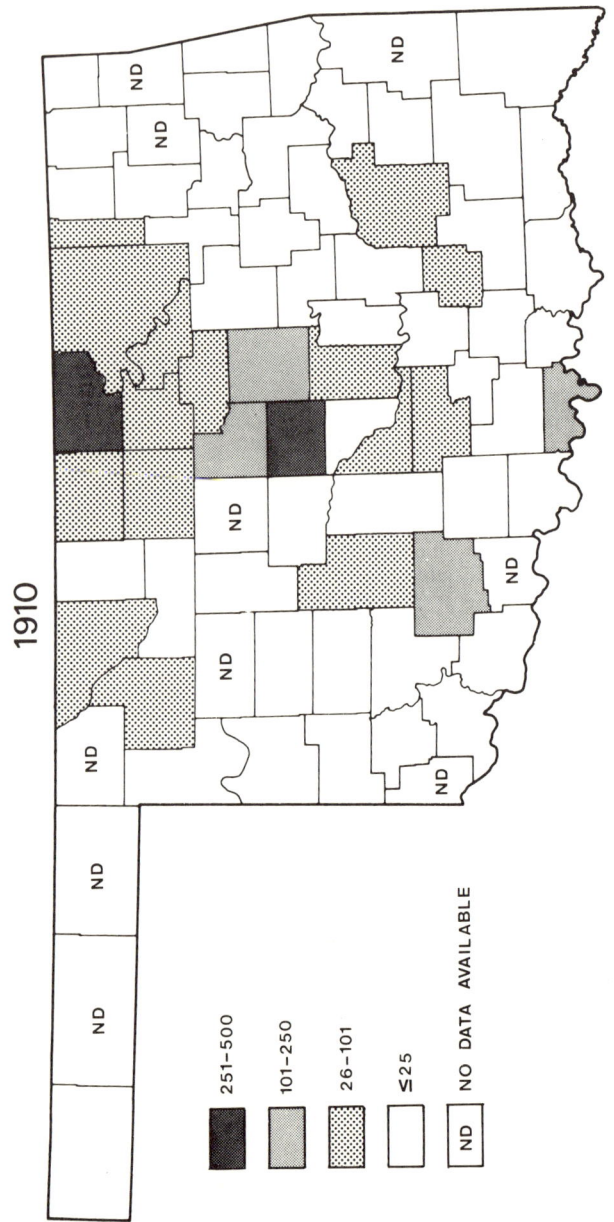

NUMBER OF OKLAHOMA RESIDENTS BORN IN MEXICO, BY COUNTY

1910

251–500

101–250

26–101

≤25

ND NO DATA AVAILABLE

Source: U. S. Census.

NUMBER OF OKLAHOMA RESIDENTS BORN IN MEXICO, BY COUNTY

1920

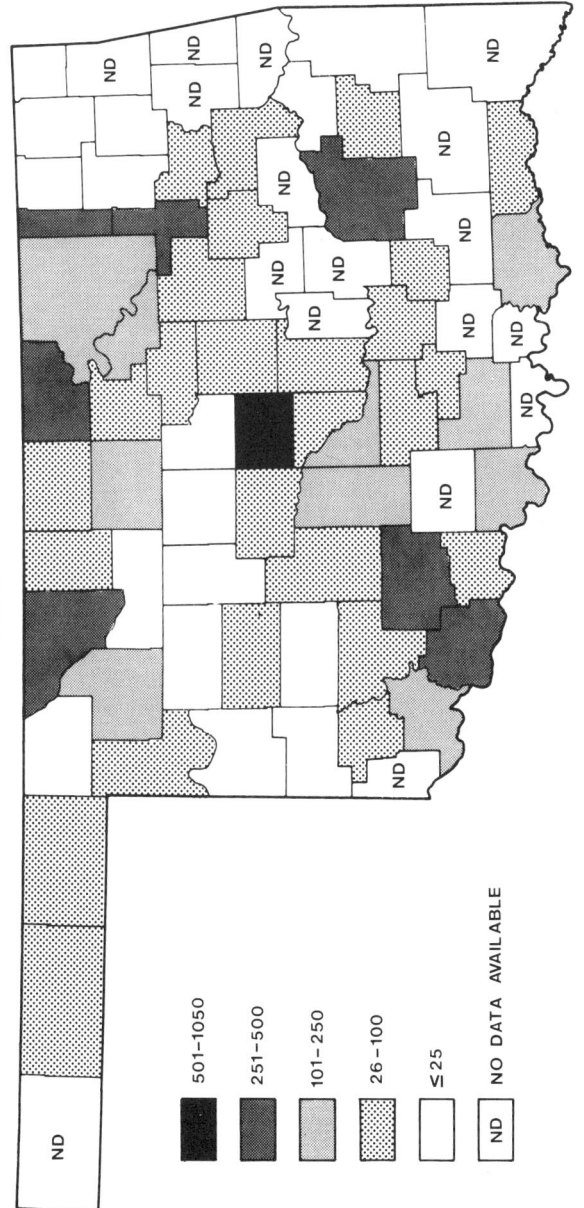

501–1050

251–500

101–250

26–100

≤25

ND   NO DATA AVAILABLE

Source: U. S. Census.

NUMBER OF MEXICANS RESIDING IN OKLAHOMA , BY COUNTY

1930

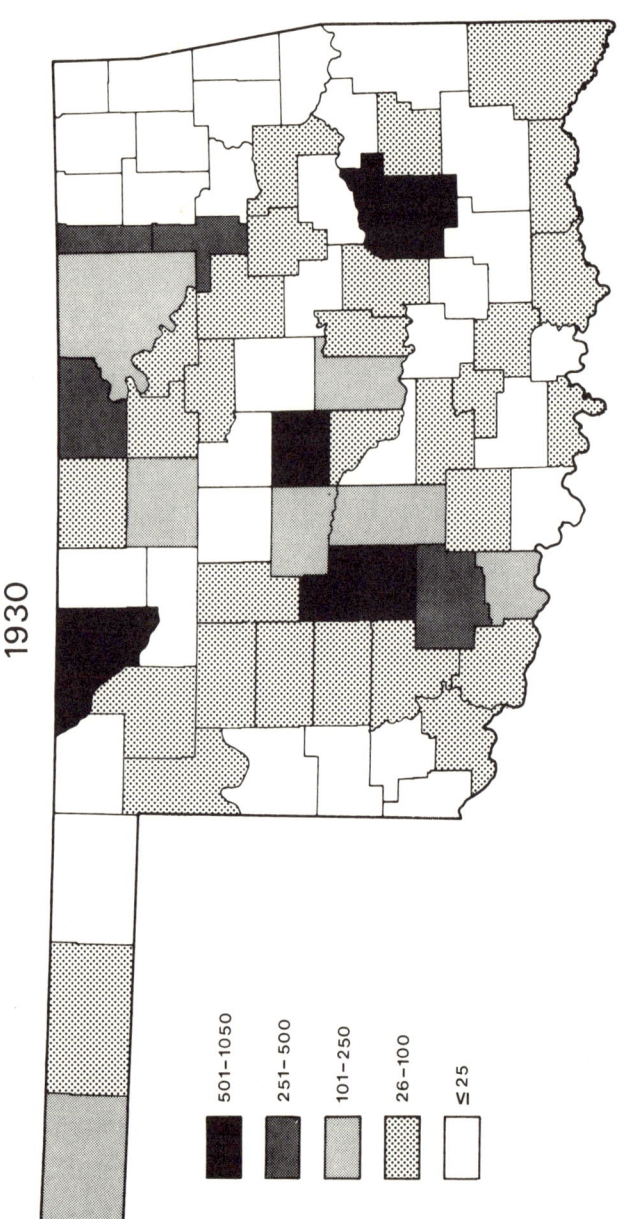

501–1050

251– 500

101–250

26–100

≤ 25

Source: U. S. Census.

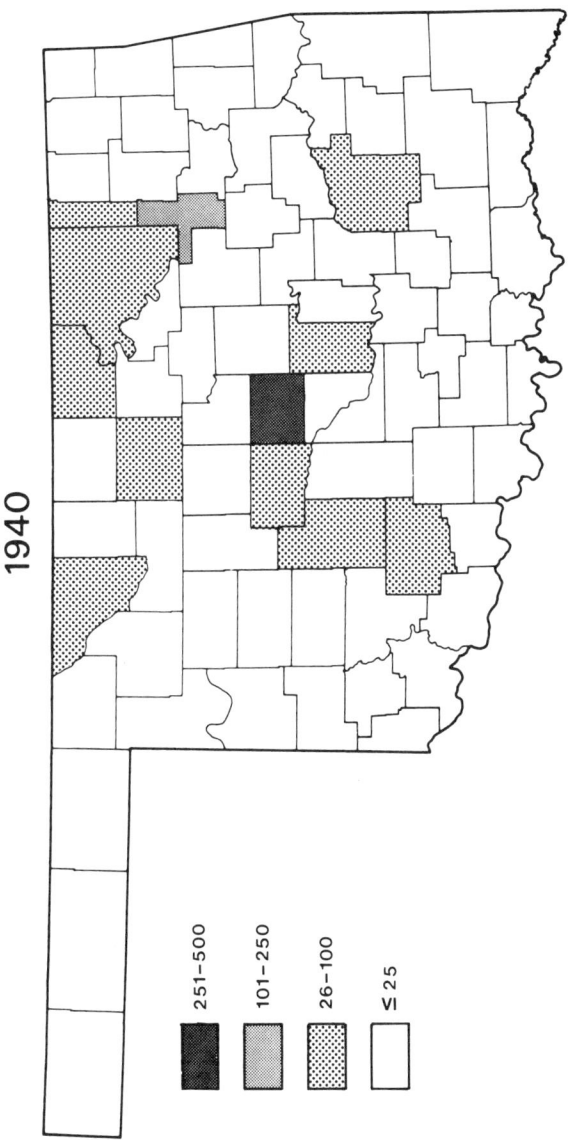

NUMBER OF OKLAHOMA RESIDENTS BORN IN MEXICO, BY COUNTY
1940

251–500

101–250

26–100

≤ 25

Source: U. S. Census.

Tulsa (346), Pittsburg (343), Tillman (295), Washington (270), Woods (253), and Bryan (250). In response to the increasing number of Mexicans who entered Oklahoma in search of employment, in 1921 the Mexican government opened a consulate in Oklahoma City. The first consul, José Montmayor, indicated that one of his major duties would be to handle any problems that arose concerning Mexican labor. The consulate also would make an effort to regulate the number of Mexicans coming to Oklahoma in order to avoid a surplus of labor. The Mexican consulate remained in Oklahoma City until the mid-1960s, when its duties were assumed by the consulate in Dallas.[11]

By 1930 the number of Mexican-born residents of Oklahoma already reflected the early stages of the depression. A total of 7,345 Mexicans, including 3,496 born in Mexico (a decline of 48 percent) and 3,849 second-generation Mexicans, lived in the state. The largest proportion of men were still employed on section gangs or as miners. The heaviest concentration of Mexicans remained in Oklahoma City, where 988 resided. In addition, over one thousand Mexicans lived in the coal-mining counties, with over eight hundred in Pittsburg County alone. Tulsa contained 294 Mexicans. Those counties with the highest number of Mexicans were Oklahoma (1,047), Pittsburg (821), Caddo (690), Woods (658), Tulsa (486), Kay (414), and Comanche (404).[12]

The depression greatly affected the presence of Mexicans in the state. Only 1,425 Mexican-born residents were recorded in 1940. Thousands had either returned to Mexico or joined the *colonias* in Los Angeles, Detroit, Chicago, and elsewhere. Employment on railroad gangs declined considerably. The Mexican population of Pittsburg County dropped 90 percent, and the Mexican-born population of Oklahoma City shrank by two-thirds. Those who remained in the state, however, endured the hardships of the depression and established the foundations of a lasting Mexican community in Oklahoma.[13]

Typically, Mexican immigrants in Oklahoma passed through El Paso or Laredo, where they often signed contracts to work on the railroads or in cotton fields. Many accompanied their parents, very likely after the father had made several seasonal trips to the state and decided to return for more permanent settlement. Perhaps they came to join relatives who had already gained employment and extolled the opportunities awaiting them north of the border. Some came to escape the violence of the revolution. Others moved to Oklahoma after having worked in the coal mines, the ranches, the beet fields, or grain farms of Texas, Colorado, Kansas, Iowa, Illinois, Indiana, or Nebraska. Occasionally an immigrant arrived by accident. One present resident of Broken Arrow related that he and some cousins had been working on the railroad in San Luis Potosí. In 1923 they came north to Texas for a vacation, ran out of money in San Antonio, went to work in a coal mine, and ultimately reached Oklahoma, where they settled permanently. The Mexican immigrants seldom found year-round employment and were forced to travel frequently, often with large families, in search of a job that usually no one else wanted. They were criticized for their nomadic existence, for their failure to take root. But the transient character of the Mexicans' way of life was seldom of their own choosing. It merely reflected the nature of the work available to them.

Gregorio Martínez was born on an *hacienda* in San Luis Potosí in 1888. While he was still a small child, his family moved to the Hacienda San Marcos near Noria de Angeles, Zacatecas. He began to work while he was a small child; for his first job as a *pastor* tending goats, he earned twelve centavos a day. When he was older, he joined the regular work crews on the *hacienda*. His tasks included tilling the fields, building fences, tending animals, and general maintenance work. He worked from dawn until dusk for twenty-five centavos a day. He still has bitter memories of life on the *hacienda*. The men, he said, were "treated like animals" and "all were slaves to their work."

In 1906 he left the *hacienda* and got a job on a section gang of the Mexican Central Railroad. In 1910 he was working from "sunrise to sunset" for sixty centavos a day. Shortly after the revolution began, he returned to the *hacienda* and married. His lot was that of the typical *peón;* he had indebted himself to start his own household. Then, in 1914 Pancho Villa's army, fresh from the stunning victory at Torreón, advanced south into Zacatecas to lay siege to the capital city. The presence of the revolutionaries caused much confusion in the countryside and disrupted life on the *hacienda*. Out of work and nearly starving, Martínez joined Villa's Division of the North as a cavalryman under the command of General Toribio Melitón Ortega. He was moved by no particular ideology or commitment to either Villa or the revolution. The army paid one and one-half pesos a day and gave him a rifle, a uniform, a horse, and provisions. After the taking of Zacatecas, Martínez (accompanied by his wife and infant son) moved on with the army to Mexico City, which Villa and Emiliano Zapata had jointly occupied. Later, when Villa returned to Chihuahua, Martínez's regiment encamped in Aguascalientes.

In 1915 Villa dueled with Venustiano Carranza for supremacy within the revolutionary movement. The Division of the North then returned to the central plateau and met Carranza's most capable general, Alvaro Obregón, at Celaya, Guanajuato. Here, wave after wave of Villa's army was slaughtered in massive assaults against Obregón's barbed-wire-protected trenches and machine guns. When Martínez learned that his regiment had been ordered to support Villa, he decided to desert. Late one night, leaving the horse and all their belongings behind, his family slipped out of the camp and returned to Zacatecas. He later found employment on the railroad again and made his way to San Luis Potosí. One evening at a railroad station he met a man who persuaded him to migrate to the United States.

The Martínez family accompanied the man and his own family on the train to Ciudad Juárez. They arrived at night, without money, food, clothes, or a place to stay. That same evening they slipped *"de contrabando"* into El Paso. He worked for a time as a mason's helper and then for a year and a half contracted several times to work on the Texas Pacific and Southern Pacific railroads. In 1917 he got a job in the Dolese Brothers quarry in Richards Spur, Oklahoma; a year later he signed on as a section hand with the Santa Fe and moved to Oklahoma City. Always employed by short term contracts, he worked variously with the Santa Fe, Frisco, and Katy railroads. When there was no track work, he picked cotton in Oklahoma and Texas.

When World War I ended and he could not find employment, Martínez decided to take his family back to Mexico. His wife was pregnant, however, and gave birth to a daughter when they reached Lawton. A friend found him a job with the Santa Fe, and he abandoned plans to return to Mexico. He worked on the railroad and supplemented his income during dead times by picking cotton. In 1933, when the depression ended his employment with the railroad, he worked at an Oklahoma City hotel and took whatever jobs he could find in the city or on nearby farms. Occasionally he worked a few days with the WPA. He worked in the quarry in Richards Spur between 1940 and 1943, before returning to Oklahoma City to work on a Katy section gang for three years. From then until his retirement in the late 1950s, he again found employment in a hotel. He and his wife reared six children in Oklahoma; all except one were born in the state.

The story of Gregorio Martínez was similar to that of many Mexicans who came to Oklahoma. He depended largely on tem-

Born on an *hacienda* in San Luis Potosí in 1888, Gregorio Martínez fought with Pancho Villa during the Mexican Revolution and then immigrated to Oklahoma in 1917. Courtesy of Mr. Gregorio Martínez.

porary or seasonal labor and never earned much money. Unlike the majority of Mexicans who came to the state, he remained during the hard years of the depression. He returned only infrequently to his native land, but steadfastly retained his Mexican citizenship. After sixty-two years in the United States, he still considers himself *"un mexicano,"* although memories of life in his own country consist largely of being *"mal comido, mal vestido, siempre con hambre"*— poorly fed, poorly dressed, and always hungry.[14]

Chapter 4
MEXICAN LABOR IN OKLAHOMA:
1900-1945

Between 1900 and the depression, Mexican immigrants played an increasingly vital, yet largely ignored role in the economic development of Oklahoma. They perhaps comprised a majority of the railroad maintenance crews and constituted a significant segment of the labor force in coal mines. Thousands of Mexican migrants annually worked the cotton harvests. Throughout the state they held numerous unskilled positions in industries, packinghouses, municipal services, and domestic employment.

No immigrant group in American history has been so intimately tied to the railroads as the Mexican. Railways provided the major arteries of migration from Mexico, and railroad companies were the principal employers of Mexican nationals in the United States. The railroads brought thousands of Mexicans to Oklahoma, and their routes often determined the patterns of settlement of Mexicans in the state. Between 1910 and the depression, Mexicans lived in nearly every city and important town along Oklahoma railroad lines. The companies often furnished their workers housing in tents, boxcars, or section houses along the right of way or encouraged them to live nearby, thus establishing the Mexican *colonia* "across the tracks." The large turnover rate in railroad gangs forced these corporations to draw a constant stream of workers into the country in order to maintain their crews at full strength.

Although the major portion of Oklahoma's railroad network was completed before 1907 and therefore prior to the heaviest migration of Mexicans to the state, they worked on construction crews in the 1880s and 1890s. Most of these "Mexicans" were probably *tejanos* who had entered the state as *vaqueros* on the cattle drives and remained or returned for more lucrative employment in railroad construction. They evidently worked a short time and then found other jobs or returned to Texas.[1]

After statehood, most railroads in Oklahoma were consolidated under the control of four major companies—the Atchinson, Topeka, and Santa Fe (Sante Fe), the Chicago, Rock Island, and Pacific (Rock Island), the St. Louis and San Francisco (Frisco), and the Missouri, Kansas, and Texas (Katy). All of these companies had direct or indirect connections to El Paso or Laredo and drew heavily upon the Mexican labor force there. While most of the railroads had employed European immigrants, blacks, and white Americans on the construction gangs, after 1907 they increasingly relied upon Mexicans for track maintenance. The most important recruiting center for Mexican track labor was El Paso, which had a seemingly endless supply of Mexican workers. During an eight-month period between 1907 and 1908, six El Paso companies supplied almost 16,500 Mexicans to various railroad corporations. The railroads needed track labor from February to October, and most Mexican immigrants, perhaps 95 percent, came to the United States intending to work only a short time. They signed contracts for three, six, or nine months, and, if they fulfilled their agreement, received free or reduced-rate transportation back to the border. One railway official stated that his company sent an agent to the Río Grande every spring to get men for the summer. He declared that the company had to keep its agreements with the men or it could not get any help the next year. Many Mexicans returned annually to work for the same railroad, often in the same geographical region.[2]

Mexicans initially filled positions on extra gangs. Their principal jobs were ballasting, laying ties, and ordinary pick and shovel work. Most were *solos,* bachelors or married men who had left their families behind. Some workers on extra crews did bring their families. Life on the extra gang was extremely nomadic. Laborers constantly moved to locations where emergency or temporary work was required. They repaired washed-out embankments, moved track to higher ground, laid new rails, or installed double tracks. They lived in dilapidated boxcars converted into crude living quarters and parked along sidings. These bare shelters contained few facilities, except perhaps a small cookstove. The company furnished water and fuel; the commissary provided food. The workers slept on straw or, if they were fortunate, rough bunks. Although men usually traveled alone on extra gangs, when there were women and children along, boxcars housing families would be parked at a distance from the rest to allow greater privacy.[3]

Michael M. Smith

The nature of extra-gang work caused many to break their contracts, and they drifted into other kinds of unskilled jobs. Farmers and ranchers frequently lured them away from the tracks by offering more money. In an attempt to keep their employees, railroad companies in Oklahoma paid wages that were higher than those generally available in Texas or other southwestern states. During the summer of 1907, Mexicans received $1.50 a day, but many still deserted to the grain and cotton fields when they had a chance. The turnover rate in track workers was consistently high until the depression. The Santa Fe, which in 1928 employed a total of 14,300 Mexicans nationally, had a turnover rate of 300 percent. No doubt the principal reasons for leaving railroad work was the unsteady nature of employ-

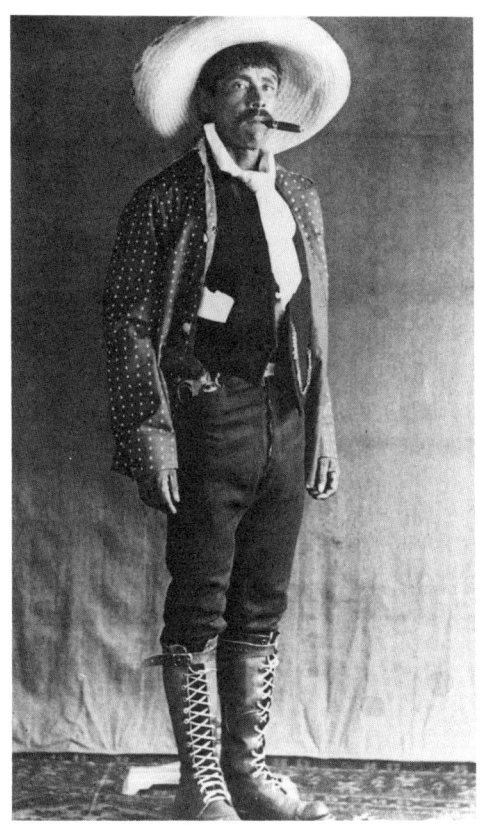

A Mexican worker who came to Oklahoma in 1899 to help construct the Eastern Oklahoma Railway's connection to Stillwater. Courtesy of the Stillwater Arts and Humanities Council.

ment, the constant moving about, and the desire of many men to be near their families.

Extra-gang employment frequently led to work on a section crew, a maintenance group assigned to a specific portion of the track line. Crews of six to thirty or more men lived in a particular community and traveled back and forth to their job on handcars. Mexicans also found employment in the railroad shops and roundhouses. Although these jobs were only semipermanent at best, they did lead to the establishment of some of the first Mexican communities in Oklahoma.

In the early years the assessment of the quality of Mexicans' work on the railroads was often unfavorable. In 1908 some railroad officials complained that Mexicans lacked ambition, were irregular in shop attendance, and drank hard after paydays, thereby losing part of their working time. Other sources, however, reported the Mexicans compared favorably with other nationalities in most respects and surpassed them in performance. Later evaluations of Mexican labor were more favorable. A Rock Island engineer listed several disadvantages of Mexican workers, including their inability to speak English, their status as temporary immigrants, and their difficulty in acclimating to harsh winters. But their refusal to be clannish, excellence as gang laborers, ability to do a full day's work in a hot climate, and faithfulness made them perhaps the best of all foreign workers. A Santa Fe official agreed that the Mexican laborers as a whole were about as steady as could be obtained for the price. He also noted that when they first arrived in this country many Mexicans were weak and malnourished. After they had been here for a month or so, however, they regained their strength and made commendable workers.

Mexican railroad laborers in Oklahoma did not experience the wage discrimination or physical abuse that their countrymen often suffered in the southwestern or Pacific states. In 1911 Mexicans were the lowest paid of any ethnic group of maintenance workers in the Pacific and Rocky Mountain regions. Over 90 percent of the Mexican workers received less than $1.50 a day. Beyond that area, however, Mexicans earned a wage comparable to that of any ethnic group. Mexican laborers earned at least $1.50 a day in Oklahoma in 1907; in the 1920s they received an average of $2.50 to $2.80 for an eight-hour day. Many Mexicans did complain of mistreatment. The Southern Pacific and the Union Pacific railroads received much criticism for their abusive handling of Mexican laborers. The Santa Fe, which probably employed the largest number of Mexicans in Oklahoma, enjoyed a generally good reputation because of its greater consideration for Mexican employees and also because it paid well. A Santa Fe engineer in the 1920s intimated that anyone who knew how to manage Mexicans could get more work out of them than any other class. A general foreman writing an article on "How to Handle Mexican Labor" stated that when properly managed, they were willing to do a great deal for their boss even if they received ridiculously low wages. In one respect, the Mexican worker in Oklahoma suffered a great disadvantage. He seldom advanced beyond the status of an extra- or section-gang member. Companies rarely hired Mexicans as foremen or assigned them the better jobs in roundhouses or repair shops. The usual reason given was that the Mexicans did not speak English well enough or did not possess the requisite skills.[4]

By 1913 the Mexicans' predominance on railroad gangs forced Santa Fe officials to make an effort to overcome the language difference between Anglo foremen and Mexican track workers. Noting that almost all the section work on its line was done by *hombres,* the Santa Fe issued foremen Spanish-English dictionaries to assist them in giving orders to their Mexican crews. Although a few Americans of Mexican descent served as foremen and most Anglo bosses spoke some Spanish, the dictionary would aid those of the latter group who had not mastered the "tongue twisters."[5]

By the outbreak of the Mexican Revolution, railroad companies such as the Santa Fe were already endeavoring to retain Mexican workers on a more permanent basis as a result of both the scarcity of track workers in general and the positive performance of Mexicans in western divisions. To attract a better and steadier class of workers, the company began to build housing for its employees so that those with families could locate on each railroad section. Santa Fe officials noted that the seminomadic life of the homeless workers encouraged the development of a vagrant class much like the American hobo. The company also noted that while many Mexicans in the western area built dugouts or tie houses with mud roofs, the earth beyond the arid region did not endure like adobe. After a heavy rain washed away the roofs of their crude shacks, many workers abandoned both the dwelling and their job.

In 1912 the Santa Fe began to erect houses on railroad property and rented them to employees for a minimal charge of one or two dollars a month. These houses were generally constructed of scrap pieces and cheap, secondhand material. Builders utilized sawed or hewn railroad ties for walls, old rails for rafters, and sheet metal for roofs. Mud or concrete filled the cracks and interstices. The dwellings did not contain furniture, plumbing, or electrical facilities. The company did provide coal, water, and stoves for heating in winter.[6]

Not all railroads supplied even these bare shelters. The first Mexicans who worked on the Frisco line in Tulsa lived in tents pitched along the right of way. The firemen on the locomotives often cast them their quota of coal as the train passed. The companies encouraged workers who did not live along the right of way to settle nearby. They preferred that the labor force reside in a compact settlement so that the entire crew of a particular section could be summoned immediately in an emergency such as a washout or derailment at night.

Until the depression and even after, the needs of the railroads dictated the distribution of many Mexicans in Oklahoma. These settlements varied considerably in size and location. They included small groups of Mexicans at such places as Blackwell, Edmond, Purcell, Pauls Valley, and Ardmore along the Santa Fe, or Medford, Enid, El Reno, Chickasha, Duncan, and Waurika beside the Rock Island. Many more worked on a large section crew or in a roundhouse in Oklahoma City, Sapulpa, or Tulsa.

A position on a section gang did not provide year-round or permanent employment. Many Mexicans in Oklahoma accepted the offer of free passage to the border and returned to Mexico after fulfilling their contract. Others saw little advantage in going home and sought alternate jobs until the railroads needed them again. A large number of railroad employees worked the cotton harvest, which began almost coincidentally with the termination of their contract period. Some found work in coal mines and industries, on farms and ranches, or as municipal employees. Numerous Mexicans had to join the great migrant agricultural pool. Families packed their few belongings and followed the sugar beet, tomato, strawberry, wheat, peach, or cranberry harvests to Kansas, Nebraska, Colorado, Iowa, Illinois, Michigan, and elsewhere.

The depression dramatically affected the employment of Mexicans on the railroads. Pressured by federal officials, labor unions, and unemployed citizens, corporations drastically reduced the number of Mexican track laborers or eliminated them entirely. The experience of the Mexican *colonia* in Sand Springs revealed the impact of the economic crisis on Mexican railroad workers. In 1917 about sixty Mexicans and their families moved to Sand Springs to construct the Sand Springs Railway. A large proportion of the men came from the coal mines in southeastern Oklahoma. The company provided "shotgun houses" near the roundhouse for the men and their families. After the railroad was completed, many remained as maintenance laborers while others found employment as section hands or in the shops or roundhouses of the Santa Fe or Frisco in Tulsa or Sapulpa. When the depression struck, they were given the option of staying in the houses which had been built for them or accepting a free pass to the border or anywhere in the United States they wished to go. Those who chose to remain would receive free rent and utilities and a few days' work a month on the railroad. Only the Fabela, Rodríguez, and Ramírez families accepted the offer and stayed.[7]

The Oklahoma coal mines also attracted a large number of Mexican immigrants. The most important coal beds lay in the old Choctaw lands, principally in Pittsburg County, and contained extensive deposits of unusually hard bituminous coal. The railroads opened the area in the 1870s, constructing numerous lines throughout the region and facilitating the development of such communities as McAlester, Krebs, Haileyville, Hartshorne, Coalgate, Lehigh, Dow, Wilburton, Henryetta, Savanna, and others. At first the towns were merely appendages of the mines. They were located a long way from developed population centers. The companies owned the houses and stores, paid their workers in scrip, and deducted one dollar a month from miners' wages for the services of a physician.

The first miners were Americans or English-speaking immigrants from Pennsylvania, Illinois, or other older mining regions. As production operations expanded, other immigrant groups including Italians, Poles, Lithuanians, Slavs, and Mexicans came to the mining district. Miners found steady employment, usually nine and a half hours a day, 250 to 300 days a year, but they labored under extremely poor conditions. The mining companies tried to extract the coal in the fastest and cheapest possible way. They invested little capital in machinery or safety equipment. Miners frequently stood in water and had to work stooped over or kneeling down to reach the narrow veins of coal. Coal dust and powder smoke filled the poorly ventilated working areas. The companies paid only for lump coal produced; the miners received nothing for "slack," or coal fragments.

The onerous working conditions led to a series of strikes between 1890 and 1895. Several trainloads of English-speaking miners blamed for inciting the disorders were sent out of the Territory and were replaced by immigrants. In 1898 miners established District Twenty-one of the United Mine Workers of America and struck again. In 1903 the companies recognized the union, granted an eight-hour day, established a pay scale of seventy-two cents per ton of coal mined, refrained from automatically deducting a physician's fee from laborers' wages, and consented to pay workers twice a month.[8]

Mexicans first began working in the Oklahoma coal fields in 1890, when they left railroad construction crews and found better pay in the mines. Later many came from Texas, where they had been employed on the railroads or in the lignite fields in the northeastern part of the state. Others came directly from the coal, silver, and copper mines of Mexico. By 1911 there were several hundred Mexicans in the coal-mining area, including about one hundred in Lehigh and another 150 in Coalgate. In later years, Mexicans scattered throughout the coal district in such places as McAlester, Hartshorne, Dow, Gowen, and Wilburton. Mexicans comprised the fourth largest ethnic group in the region, exceeded only by the number of Italians, Poles, and Lithuanians. More than half of the "Mexicans" were *tejanos,* but authorities reported that they were no more Americanized than those who had come directly from Mexico.

An Immigration Commission study of the Oklahoma coal-mining region in 1911 indicated that Mexican-born miners had resided longer in the United States than had their countrymen who worked in track maintenance. In that year about 25 percent had lived in this country from five to nine years, 25 percent from ten to fourteen years, and 20 percent from fifteen to nineteen years. Slightly less than 10 percent had resided twenty or more years in the United States. Nearly 50 percent of the men had been miners in Mexico, while about 30 percent had worked as farm laborers.

Coal mining was the only industry employing large amounts of labor in the region at that time, and few opportunities for work outside the mines existed. One hundred percent of the Mexican workers in the district held jobs in the coal mines. Most Mexicans worked between six and nine months a year, averaging 172 work days annually. Much of the time lost was the result of the usual suspension of production from April to June. During these slack times, most Mexicans sought work on the railroad crews and then returned when the mines resumed operations.

The two basic classes of employees in the mines were pieceworkers and day men (or company men). Pieceworkers received a specific sum for each ton of coal that they produced. Day men worked for a fixed daily wage and held the more responsible or skilled jobs as mule drivers, fire runners, gasmen, trackmen, hoisting engineers, or bratticers. Only Americans or English-speaking immigrants held company positions. All Mexicans, whom the company officials deemed unsuitable for other tasks, were employed as pieceworkers. Most Mexicans, however, preferred piecework because industrious miners could earn more money than the day men.[9]

In the early 1900s about one-third of the mines were of the vertical shaft type, which ultimately reached a depth of from seventy to 800 feet. The other two-thirds were slope or drift mines with an incline that ranged from fifty to thirty-five hundred feet in length. Mines of either class depended exclusively upon pickmining techniques. This type of mining usually required two-man work teams. The "buddies" worked in the same room, often over a period of several years. One man did the mining and placed the powder; the other loaded the coal on the cars. They often worked one hundred feet or more from the entry, isolated from the other miners. The only other employee they saw during the day was the driver who brought the empty cars and took away the full ones. As a result of this isolated, prolonged personal contact, miners uniformly preferred to work with a member of their own ethnic group—Mexicans worked with Mexicans. It was not unusual for fathers and sons, brothers, close relatives, or *compadres* to work as partners.[10]

In 1911 Mexicans earned an average daily wage of $2.46, the lowest of all immigrant groups surveyed. Observers stated that Mexicans generally were not as physically strong as other immigrants and therefore were unable to mine as much coal on a daily basis. All Mexicans, however, earned at least $1.50 per day, while slightly less than 10 percent earned over $3.00. The Mexican miner's average annual income was about $379, but a few earned over $600 per year. Almost all Mexican families had to supplement the father's wages. In some cases children worked in the mines and contributed all or a portion of their income for family expenses. About 20 percent of the Mexican households kept lodgers or boarders, and women frequently took in washing and ironing from the single Mexican men. No Mexican women, however, worked in any capacity outside the home. Including all sources of income, the average Mexican family earned about $470 a year.[11]

Miners were paid in cash every two weeks. Although most companies operated a store, employees could purchase their goods wherever they chose. In some instances, however, the company store was the only business establishment near the mine, and workers were forced to patronize it. Between paydays no miners received cash. The only way they could get supplies when they had no cash was to draw scrip or get orders on credit at the company store. The amount of the purchase which the miners made with scrip or on credit was deducted from their wages on payday.

Life was generally difficult for the Mexican miners and their families. The Immigration Commission report noted that Mexicans were the poorest of all immigrant groups in the mining area. The vast majority lived in two- or three-room company houses. Located near the mines and arranged in one or more rows, depending upon the size of the operation, these cheap, poorly constructed dwellings were usually painted a dull red and almost always needed repairs. Their flooring was poor; only a few had ceilings. Most were unfinished inside, and in all the houses, windows and doors fit improperly. Often the structures were elevated two or three feet above the ground, with the corners resting unsteadily on piles of bricks or rocks. Several families shared a well for drinking water; outdoor toilets stood at a distance from the dwellings.

Most miners rented private houses or purchased their own homes as soon as they could. The poverty of the Mexicans, however, forced them to remain in the company houses. They paid an average rent of $1.65 a room per month, a sum deducted from their wages. These houses consisted of little more than bare rooms with no furniture except a cooking stove. Residents slept on rude bunks or straw strewn on the floor. Because Mexicans had large families and because they often shared their quarters with relatives or lodgers, their homes were the most congested in the mining region. It was often necessary to utilize every room in the house, including the kitchen, to provide sleeping space for all inhabitants.[12]

The Immigration Commission report was highly critical of the Mexicans in the coal-mining region. Its statement was a litany of shortcomings. Fewer Mexicans than any other group—22 percent of the men and 15 percent of the women—spoke English. They stubbornly maintained their Mexican citizenship and demonstrated a decided lack of "civic responsibility." A survey of Pittsburg, Okmulgee, Coal, and Latimer counties revealed that not a single Mexican immigrant had taken any steps toward naturalization. They showed a strong disinclination to mix with Americans, perhaps because, as the study noted, they were "heartily disliked by natives." They did not send their children to school; only four Mexican children were attending classes in the nine communities examined. Mexicans were improvident; they usually stopped working after payday and would not return until the money was spent. Mexicans were too migratory; they often moved from one coal mine to another and almost never acquired property. Investigators concluded that Mexicans "showed less progress towards Americanization" than any other immigrant group. Those born in the United States were as little inclined to become Americanized as those from Mexico.[13]

Between 1910 and the depression, the Mexican population in the mining areas showed continuous growth. Although most Mexicans resided in Pittsburg County—eighty-six in 1910, 343 in 1920, and 821 in 1930—they also worked in Coal, Latimer, and Tulsa counties. Many Mexicans had migrated to Oklahoma from Trinidad, Colorado, or from the lignite fields of Alba and Malakoff, Texas, where Mexicans comprised the vast majority of miners. When Mexicans found satisfactory employment, they sent for their families and convinced relatives and friends to join them. Members of the Casillas family of Tulsa, who came originally from Purísima del Rincón, Guanajuato, worked in the mines of Colorado and Texas before finding employment east of Tulsa with the Old Hickory and Scales Mining companies in the 1920s.[14]

Oklahoma coal mines were among the most dangerous in the United States; coal mining had the highest fatality rate of any major industry in the state. As miners pushed shafts and slopes deeper underground, disasters caused by coal dust or gas explosions, poorly placed or overpowdered shots, fires, bad ventilation, and cave-ins took a rising toll of lives. Occasionally a Mexican miner distinguished himself for his bravery; frequently, Mexican families suffered the anguish of the crippling injury or death of a loved one.

On February 22, 1912, twenty-two-year-old Rufino Rodríguez, an illiterate Mexican coal miner working at Lehigh's Number Five Mine, saved 190 fellow workers from certain death after a fire broke out about one hundred feet from the bottom of the shaft. Rather than flee to save his own life, Rodríguez fought through the suffocating smoke and sounded the alarm throughout the interior of the mine. He ran from entry to entry alerting the miners and helping men who were struggling and suffocating in the darkness of the shaft. He fell unconscious near the main entry, where fellow workers pulled him to safety. Ten men lost their lives in the disaster, but Rodríguez's efforts had enabled 190 more to escape. Miners in Lehigh voted him a gift of one hundred dollars. The union pledged to pay for his education at any school of his choosing and recommended him to the Carnegie Foundation for a citation of bravery. In May 1914, Rodríguez received a bronze medal for heroism from the Carnegie Hero Fund Commission.[15]

On a more tragic note, on December 17, 1929, thirty-two Mexican miners died when a spark from one of the electric cutting machines ignited a gas explosion in the Old Town Company's Little Bolen Mine at McAlester. Sixty-one of the sixty-six men working below were burned to death, blown to bits, or overcome by gas. Rescue teams entered the mine to search for bodies while Red Cross workers and volunteers from the local American Legion post aided a company of national guardsmen in keeping order. Grief-stricken families watched in stoical silence as rescuers carried the bodies to makeshift morgues. Only miners were admitted to identify the remains.

The disaster claimed five sets of brothers—all Mexicans. They worked in the mine together and died together. The dead included Gregorio, Alberto, and Juan Chávez; Francisco and Edúviges Medina; Alberto and Luis Pérez; Francisco and Alberto Moreno; and Nick and Tino Cisneros. Valentín Cisneros, who had worked in the mines for fifty years, watched as his two remaining sons helped bring out their brothers' bodies. He betrayed no outward emotion when he learned that his sons were dead. "I have two left," he said simply. "If I had more, they would be miners too."

Red Cross officials coordinating the relief noted that almost 250 women, children, and old men left behind by the miners faced hunger, cold, a cheerless Christmas, and a dismal future. People from Oklahoma and across the nation donated over $75,000 to the McAlester relief fund. Will Rogers sent a check for $1,000, and the Mexican government contributed $10,000 to aid destitute Mexican families. On December 20, a Catholic priest officiated at the mass burial of twenty-four of the Mexicans; eight others were buried in separate services. Surviving dependents did not have the benefits of death insurance, which was forbidden by state law. It was reported that frequently after mine disasters, company officials told widows and orphans, "We can't pay damages; the mine is wrecked; take the mine if you wish!"[16]

The years between 1903 and 1922 were prosperous ones for the Oklahoma coal-mining industry. During World War I, labor was in short supply, wages were high, and double shifts could not produce enough coal. The average daily wage rose from $2.56 in 1903 to $3.60 in 1917 and to $7.50 in 1925. By 1922, however, the mining industry began to decline. The wartime economic boom peaked and then receded; fuel oil and natural gas began to replace coal in many industries and communities. A severe strike hit the coal fields between 1924 and 1927. Companies imported strikebreakers, defeated

Mass Burial of twenty-four Mexican miners killed in the McAlester mine disaster, December 1929. Courtesy of the Western History Collections, University of Oklahoma.

the union, and forced an open shop. During the strike, twelve hundred Mexicans served as breakers for the five-dollar wages that the companies were offering. Six hundred Mexicans worked in McAlester — some of whom certainly died in the disaster of 1929. Another six hundred scattered throughout the mining district. Wages remained at five dollars a day until 1931, when they dropped to $3.60 and as low as $2.00. Miserable working conditions and wage cuts sparked strikes in 1931 and 1932. Mexicans joined the union and supported American labor leaders. But when the full impact of the depression struck the area, most Mexicans abandoned the mines, moved to Tulsa or Oklahoma City in search of other employment, or simply left the state.[17]

The Mexicans in Oklahoma

Mexicans played an important role in Oklahoma agriculture, especially in their capacity as migrant or temporary cotton pickers. An observer reported that two kinds of Mexicans engaged in the cotton harvest. Many immigrants were making their first, or possibly second or third, seasonal visit to the United States. They had crossed the border east of El Paso and found employment on railroads, ranches, or farms in Texas before migrating to Oklahoma. The other group consisted of a large number of American or Mexican frontier residents who lived along the border and resided intermittently in either country. Many of these people had worked in Oklahoma as early as the 1890s and returned each year during the cotton harvest. They annually joined a large labor force that followed a circuit from south Texas, to Oklahoma, to the cane fields of Louisiana, and then back to Texas. It was not unusual for Oklahoma cotton growers to send a manager or foreman to the Río Grande to recruit a party of one hundred or more men and their families. They preferred, however, simply to offer higher wages than the railroads paid. They could then draw Mexicans from the section gangs and save the cost of railway fare or other recruiting expenses.[18]

Cotton production expanded rapidly in Oklahoma after 1907, especially in the western part of the state where the relatively level plains enable growers to utilize more machinery. A farmer could grow more cotton than his family and local labor could pick. *Tejanos* and Mexicans therefore supplied a major portion of the seasonal labor force. In 1907 a worker could earn from fifty to seventy-five cents for every one hundred pounds of cotton he picked; by 1925 pickers earned as much as two dollars per hundred. The large number of Mexicans engaged in picking cotton in Oklahoma was highlighted during the depression when nativist writers sought to restrict the employment of Mexicans. One author stated that on the plains of Texas and Oklahoma millions of acres previously used as ranges for cattle, sheep, and goats had been turned over to cotton cultivation. Here, Mexican tenants or hired workers living in miserable shacks toiled for non-resident landlords.

Certainly living conditions during the *pizca* (as Mexicans called the cotton harvest) were primitive. Large families, often with ten or more children, lived in tents, rude shacks, or canvas-covered carts. They lacked adequate sources of water and even the most elementary sanitation facilities. All members of the family who were able to work—including small children—joined the harvest. A family unit commonly could pick from 200 to 300 pounds of cotton a day.

Michael M. Smith

Mexicans at Post Oak Mission, Comanche County. Courtesy of the Western History Collections, University of Oklahoma.

Although some Mexicans were sharecroppers or tenants before the depression, few ever owned their own farms. Most Mexicans either returned to Texas or Mexico or signed on again with the railroad after the harvest. Around such areas as Anadarko and Lawton, where Mexicans worked Indian lands, it was not unusual for a Mexican to marry an Indian woman and acquire property in that way.

While Oklahoma farmers often did not accept Mexicans as individuals, they did deem their labor both necessary and preferable to that of other groups. In 1930, when many Americans demanded the prohibition of Mexican workers, an Oklahoma onion grower offered the following assessment of the Mexicans he employed: "They don't work, but they increase like rats. If something is not done we will soon be shoved out of the picture. There ought to be a law passed that every [white] married couple should have so many children and if they don't, they ought to find out why." He went on to say that he "would be blowed up if they stopped immigration. The scarcity of labor makes me pay what my crop is worth to get it harvested. . . . The white people I could get at a reasonable price I wouldn't want. I prefer Mexicans."

Mexicans found employment in a variety of occupations before the depression. They worked in the lumber mills of southeastern

David B. Zamudio and his tamale cart. Courtesy of the Western History Collections, University of Oklahoma.

Oklahoma and in the oil fields of Bartlesville; in gravel pits and quarries in Richards Spur and Dewey. They built roads and streets and dug sewer and gas lines in Tulsa and Lawton. And they worked in the mills at Shawnee and Enid. As Bishop Francis C. Kelley would note later, "Mexicans in Oklahoma [were] mostly employed like other residents but in poorer positions."

The depression years were severe times for Mexicans in the state. Many had come during or after World War I and had little time to adjust to American culture. Unquestionably most had arrived penniless, and a majority lived on the edge of poverty even in good times. Mexicans were usually classified as temporary residents. Most had taken no steps toward naturalization, and only a slight fraction had become American citizens. Frequently they did not speak or read English; even those born in the United States often did not read or write the language. Although the extreme hostility and segregation Mexicans experienced in Texas were not as severe in Oklahoma, racial prejudice was always present. When most Americans found it difficult to survive the crisis—witness the thousands of "Okies" who fled the state—it was understandable that few Mexicans could endure the tribulations of the period.

While thousands returned to Mexico or migrated to other states, some stubbornly resolved to remain in Oklahoma. At times they barely survived. Many collected and sold old bottles, paper, coal, or scrap metal, in order to feed their large families. Often they were too proud to accept charity and refused relief services. Others relied heavily on the family garden, raised a few animals, or hunted game. Although federal law prohibited the employment of aliens in the New Deal relief programs, some Mexicans "passed" as Indians and found occasional work with such projects as the WPA. Others became gardeners and worked around the grounds of the more prosperous citizens. Almost every sizable Oklahoma town had its tamale vendor. Mexican women would grind the corn that they had raised in the family garden and make the tamales. The men packed their products into a handcart and peddled them wherever they could. Some families who opened Mexican restaurants after prosperity returned had gotten their start in the food business with the humble tamale cart.[19]

Chapter 5

SOCIAL AND CULTURAL ADJUSTMENTS: 1900-1945

Mexican-born residents of Oklahoma between 1900 and 1945 had left behind a powerful folk culture that had governed their lives in Mexico and would continue to exert great influence upon them in this country.[1] Although Mexicans of all classes and backgrounds migrated to Oklahoma after 1900, the large majority were *campesinos;* many had been *peones.* They had lived in a neo-feudalistic society in which a change in status was virtually impossible. In Mexico they had no land or power; they seldom aspired to achieve either. They tended to accept their position and preferred to persevere and survive rather than attempt to change the system. The Mexican village offered an emotionally secure world of patriarchal, extended families in which everyday acquaintances were familiar and everyone's role in society was recognized. The paternalistic nature of the *patrón-peón* relationship continued to affect their attitudes toward employers and those in authority in this country. The early evaluation of the Mexican workers as unambitious, docile, and obedient clearly reflected their cultural background. When Mexicans confronted the indifferent, competitive, and changing character of American life, the gulf between the two cultures made adjustment and assimilation a difficult, often impossible, process.[2]

A major impediment to Mexicans' adjustment to American culture was their inability to speak or read English; indeed, a large majority were illiterate in Spanish. Their society did not encourage or financially support public education for the masses. As late as 1910, over 80 percent of all Mexicans were illiterate; this proportion was even greater in the rural areas. The Díaz administration established no schools for the lower classes or Indians. The typical Mexican immigrant was the product of a society that did not esteem education.

He also often had to put even his elementary-age children to work. Most Mexican immigrants understandably failed to take advantage of the educational opportunities available in the United States. In 1911 the Immigration Commission noted that Mexican children showed the lowest rate of school attendance in the Oklahoma coal-mining region. According to the United States census of 1930, Mexicans still had the smallest percentage of children in school. The low literacy rate in Spanish accounted for the lack of Spanish-language newspapers or other publications in Oklahoma. Those who wished to read newspapers in their own language usually subscribed to *La Prensa,* a Spanish-language journal published in San Antonio.

Inability to speak English often isolated Mexicans from the broader community and was a principal reason given for Mexicans' failure to get more responsible or remunerative jobs. Young children often accompanied their fathers to union meetings to translate the proceedings in Spanish. Mexican women, who acquired a knowledge of English even less frequently than did their husbands, found it extremely difficult to shop. They often had to draw pictures, engage in exaggerated pantomimes, or take along one of their children who spoke English in order to communicate with merchants. While the first generation continued to speak standard Mexican Spanish, the language which they used and which they taught their children often contained numerous Hispanicized English words and phrases, known as *pochismos.* The most common *pochismos* used in Oklahoma include *tiquete* (ticket), *mecha* (match), *carro* (car), *traque* (track), *ganga* (gang), *troque* (truck), *parquear* (to park), *huáchale* (watch it), and *púshale* (push it).

Mexicans did not generally seek citizenship in this country. In 1930, of the 320,000 Mexican-born residents in the United States who were over twenty-one years of age, only 5.5 percent (as compared with 49.7 percent of the entire foreign-born adult population) had become naturalized citizens. A number of factors mitigated against naturalization. Before the depression and World War II, few Mexicans perceived any advantage in becoming citizens. They continued to hold menial jobs, lived in inferior houses, and often encountered discrimination. Many had entered the country illegally, which precluded their acquiring citizenship. Most had come to the United States for a short time as a means of supporting their families in Mexico. Persistent economic and political problems at home often extended their stay but did not loosen their bonds of loyalty to Mexico. Unlike the European immigrant, Mexicans did not cut all ties to the homeland. They lived relatively close to the mother country, returned frequently to visit family and friends, and therefore repeatedly renewed their cultural roots. Mexicans continued to view themselves as temporary residents of the United States even though their tenure might last many years. Pressure within the community often dissuaded individuals from giving up their Mexican citizenship and adopting American ways. Proud of their native land and customs, Mexicans often resented one who became too *agringado* ("gringoized"). Those who affected the speech, dress, and customs of the *güeros* ("blonds") were derisively called *"pochos."*[3]

Even today, after spending as much as seventy years in the state, many Mexicans proudly retain their Mexican citizenship. They express love and gratitude for the opportunities this country did offer them, but still reveal a strong desire to maintain their *mexicanidad* (Mexicanism). One long-time resident stated, *"Uno es mexicano dondequiera,"* or "One is a Mexican anywhere." Another declared, *"Soy mexicano por adentro; no puedo cambiar eso,"* or "I am a Mexican inside; I can't change that."

Most Mexican immigrants—especially those of *criollo* background—agree that although there was a great deal of "separation" between Mexicans and the broader community, the acute racial prejudice and segregation that they experienced in Texas and other southwestern states was not characteristic of their treatment in Oklahoma. Mexican children were not excluded from public or parochial schools. No signs warning "No Niggers, Mexicans, or Dogs Allowed" greeted them as they attempted to patronize business establishments. Perhaps because there were relatively few Mexicans in the state, the Anglo majority did not perceive them as a threat. Unlike such places as San Antonio, Los Angeles, Kansas City, Omaha, or Chicago, Oklahoma had no large *colonias.* Even where substantial numbers did reside, such as in Oklahoma City, employment determined their settlement patterns, and the population was widely dispersed. Mexicans maintained little social contact with the Anglo majority. They were typically of mestizo descent; their dark hair and skin therefore gave them a high degree of ethnic visibility. Their use of Spanish, their different customs, and their deficiency in labor skills dictated the social milieu in which they would live.

Mexicans did encounter prejudice in the state. One man declared, *"Cuando llegamos, nos trataron como negros."* ("When we arrived, they treated us like Negroes.") Anglos often called them "dirty Mexicans" or "greasers." Another immigrant noted that when

Michael M. Smith

she entered first grade, she did not speak English. The Anglo children laughed at her because of the way she spoke and appeared. In school she and other Mexican children were required to sit together at one side of the classroom. American children would often force them off the walkways and into the street as they went home from school. Only after her older cousins began to escort them home did the taunting stop.

Immigrant *corridos* (ballads) often expressed the sentiment that Oklahoma was not a desirable place for Mexicans. These songs depicted the immigrants' experiences, folk heroes, and misfortunes. In one of these *corridos, "De las tres que vienen aí"* ("Of Three Approaching Girls"), the singer intones, "Do not send me to Texas, nor to the state of Oklahoma; they are awful places that make it hard for one who drinks"—an obvious reference to Oklahoma's prohibitionism. In another, *"Los reenganchados a Kianses"* ("Contracted to Kansas"), the balladeer sings, "I asked the Contractor if we were going to Oklahoma. The Contractor replied, 'Quiet, friend, don't even sigh. We shall pass right through Oklahoma. . . .'"[4]

In their homeland, especially in the small towns and rural areas, Mexicans neither showed much individual enterprise nor readily formed social or cooperative organizations for mutual aid. The extended family or even the *patrón* took care of their immediate needs when they experienced difficulties. In this respect, Mexicans changed considerably in the United States. A number of national or ethnic organizations were founded among immigrant groups to provide greater cohesion to the communities, serve as mutual-aid societies, or to protect the rights of Mexican immigrants and citizens of Mexican descent. Among the most important of these organizations were *La Alianza Hispano Americana* (The Hispanic American Alliance), *La Sociedad Mutualista Mexicana* (The Mexican Mutual Benefit Society), *La Comisión Honorífica* (The Honorary Commission), *La Cruz Azul* (The Blue Cross), and the League of United Latin American Citizens (LULAC).[5]

Mexican immigrant organizations established in Oklahoma included the Comisiones Honoríficas, the Cruz Azul, and the *Sociedad Benéfica Nacional* (National Benefit Society). The Comisiones Honoríficas were composed of the most respected members of the Mexican community. The Mexican consul usually served as the honorary president and collaborated with local members to oversee the welfare of immigrants in the vicinity. The Cruz Azul, which also had a women's auxiliary, served as a beneficent and mutual-aid society. Members contributed a small amount of money on a regular basis to buy flowers or help pay funeral expenses. They also provided food and clothing when Mexican immigrants and their families were in dire need. The Sociedad Benéfica Nacional had long served as a mutual benefit organization among Mexicans in the Oklahoma coal-mining region.

One of the principal functions of the immigrant societies—especially the Comisiones Honoríficas—was the organization of the *fiestas patrias* (national celebrations). The three major celebrations observed in Oklahoma were *"El 16 de Septiembre"* ("The 16th of September"), *"El Cinco de Mayo"* ("The Fifth of May"), and *"El Día de la Virgen de Guadalupe"* ("The Day of the Virgin of Guadalupe"). *"El 16 de Septiembre"* was the major celebration of the year. It marked Mexico's independence day and commemorated Father Miguel Hidalgo y Costilla's *"Grito de Dolores"* ("Cry of Dolores"), which launched the movement for independence against Spain in 1810. The *"Cinco de Mayo"* celebrated Mexico's stout defense of Puebla against the invading French army in 1862. On these festive days, the Mexican community would gather together to sing the Mexican national anthem and hear speeches and recitations. The Mexican consul frequently gave the principal address and explained the significance of the occasion. Children presented short patriotic plays depicting the deeds of the national heroes. Various groups performed the *jarabe tapatío* ("Mexican Hat Dance") and many other popular regional dances. Adults and children participated in a variety of games and enjoyed many typical Mexican dishes. Bands entertained the crowd with *mariachi* and *ranchera* music and songs. The Day of the Virgin of Guadalupe was the principal religious holiday for the Mexican community. A special mass and celebration was held on December 12 to commemorate the Virgin's appearance to Juan Diego on Tepeyac Hill outside Mexico City. All of these ceremonies enabled immigrants to maintain contact with their Mexican culture and teach children something of their historical and religious heritage.

Few social institutions served the Mexican immigrants in Oklahoma, and their own ethnic organizations possessed neither the permanence nor the power to affect significantly their status in the community. One cohesive and enduring element in the Mexicans' lives in Oklahoma was the Roman Catholic Church. At first, however, Mexicans settled where there were no Spanish-speaking priests, and their participation in church activities was greatly restricted. In addition, although Mexicans were nominally Catholic, many had been raised in a markedly anti-clerical environment. Women and children were generally devoted to religious observance, but the Mexican male seldom participated in church activities. He married in a religious service, ensured that his children were baptized and received the sacraments, and perhaps attended mass on major feast days. The distinct anti-Catholic attitudes of Oklahoma's Bible-Belt Protestantism and the Ku Klux Klan's activities in the state during the 1920s often presented difficulties for all Catholics. Ultimately, however, the Catholic church played an important role in the Mexican's life in Oklahoma as it provided both spiritual and material aid in an alien and at times hostile environment.

That segment of the Catholic church which had the closest ties to Mexican immigrants in Oklahoma was the Order of the Discalced Carmelites. In 1914 when Pancho Villa's revolutionary army captured Torreón, Coahuila, he encountered a group of Spanish Carmelites stationed there. Villa, who regarded all Spaniards as enemies of the revolution and held strong antichurch sentiments, decided to execute the three priests. After the wife of the American consul dissuaded him from this, Villa shipped the priests and a large number of other Spaniards to El Paso on a cattle train. In 1915 the three Carmelites

A group of predominantly Mexican students with a Carmelite sister and priest at Little Flower School, c. 1930. Courtesy of Father John Michael Payne, O.C.D.

were invited to establish a foundation in Oklahoma to serve the growing number of Catholics in the state. They founded a mission at Hartshorne and soon thereafter extended their activities to include other coal-mining towns such as Pittsburg, Gowen, Wilburton, Bentley, Coalgate, and Lehigh. They traveled to the towns on horseback or in wagons from which they often said mass or offered the sacraments. Although they served all Catholics in these areas, their ability to speak Spanish was of special importance to Mexican members of the communities.

In 1921 the order received permission to establish a mission in Oklahoma City to minister to the growing Mexican population in the capital city. After several years and a few severe setbacks—the menace of the Ku Klux Klan forced them to alter radically their plans to build a truly magnificent structure—the Carmelites completed Little Flower Church on South Walker Street in 1927. In addition, Carmelite nuns established Little Flower School for Mexican children in the city. Ultimately, the order added a community house, which provided instructional opportunities for Mexican families, and operated a clinic to aid the ill and poverty-stricken members of the *colonia*. Although classes in the school were taught in English, sermons and other religious and social functions were conducted in Spanish. One altar of the church was dedicated to the Virgin of Guadalupe, and every December 12 special masses and celebrations were held in the parish. Little Flower Church became and has endured as the locus of the Mexican community in Oklahoma City.[6]

When Mexican immigrants first settled in Tulsa, no church offered services in Spanish, and most Mexicans attended mass at St. Francis Church. In the early twenties, Spanish-speaking Carmelites from Oklahoma City offered mass once a month in the homes of the miners who lived east of the city. The first Spanish-language church was established in the mining camps between present-day Eleventh and Fifteenth streets. Mexican miners had received permission to convert an old company store into a church. They tore out the walls of the old structure, built an altar, and founded Our Lady of Guadalupe. In 1929, with donated materials and lumber, they constructed a larger, wood-framed church which Spanish-speaking priests continued to serve. Finally, in the forties, after the mines played out, the church was moved to its present location on East Newton Place and North Trenton. Like Little Flower Church in Oklahoma City, Our Lady of Guadalupe Church became the religious and social center for the Mexican *colonia* in Tulsa.

Despite the cushioning factor that ethnic societies and the church provided, the Mexican immigrants' race, culture, language, and economic status combined to keep the first generation separated from the larger culture. Intermarriage between Anglos and Mexicans was an almost inconceivable occurrence. Occasionally Mexicans wed Indians; even more rarely Mexicans and Negroes married. Social contact between the first generation immigrant and Anglo society was extremely rare. Although there was a harmonious relationship between the groups on the job, after working hours Mexicans associated with other Mexicans or kept to themselves. Entertainment, leisure activities, and religious services were held within the group.

Payday in the railroad sections or mining communities invariably was an occasion to have a fiesta in the home of one of the families. Families gathered, played Mexican popular and ranchera music, and danced. They enjoyed both typical Mexican dances or modified versions of the fox trot and two-step. Some had phonographs on which they played the most recent recordings. Most frequently, however, several of the men provided live music. In the mining camps of Tulsa,

A Mexican wedding party at Post Oak Mission, Comanche County. Courtesy of the Western History Collections, University of Oklahoma.

members of the Mendoza family were renowned for their musical talents, and no fiesta was complete without their participation.

First communions, confirmations, and weddings also provided occasions for celebration. In addition, fiestas were held to honor someone's *santo* ("saint's day"). In Mexico it was customary to celebrate the feast day of the particular saint after whom an individual was named. On such occasions the women made a special effort to prepare typical Mexican food. Guests enthusiastically devoured plates and bowls of *tortillas,* tamales, *enchiladas, tacos, chiles rellenos, flautas, gorditas, panuchos, empanadas, menudo, mole,* and *frijol con puerco.* To add an additional touch of flavor, they spiced the dishes with *salsas picantes* made from *chile rojo, chile verde,* or *chile ancho.*

The principal focus of the immigrants life in Oklahoma, as in Mexico, was the family. The Mexican family exhibited a high degree of solidarity and was extremely patriarchal. In the home, the father's word was law. The role of Mexican women was limited to maternal and household obligations. Women did not seek employment outside the home even under the most impoverished circumstances. Not only was it demeaning for a man's wife or daughters to work, it was a blow to his self-respect. In addition, the Mexican family severely limited women's freedom of action in other ways. Girls and young women did not go out on dates unless they were duly chaperoned.

Mexican culture placed great emphasis upon obedience to and respect and consideration for elders. Children were taught to care for their brothers and sisters. Responsibility to the family was a lifelong commitment. In old age, the elders were brought to live with their children, and the family was its own social agency whenever possible.

The Mexican family unit was greatly expanded by a system of extended kinship known as the *compadrazgo.* An individual acquired one or more *padrinos* (godparents) on several occasions of spiritual significance during his lifetime—baptism, first communion, confirmation, or marriage. By acting as a child's baptismal sponsor, for example, the *padrino* (godfather) and *madrina* (godmother) became his coparents and assumed the responsibility of caring for the spiritual and material well-being of their *ahijado* or *ahijada* (male or female godchild). The child's parents and godparents referred to each other as *compadre* (male) or *comadre* (female) and formed a close bond based upon their commitment to render mutual aid and support.

The *compadrazgo*, therefore, offered the immigrants a broader web of social relationships and provided an added measure of security within a culturally unfamiliar and economically unstable environment. The basic character of the Mexican family, however, was severely tested in American culture. Children grew up in a society which gave them greater independence and placed less importance upon obedience, respect, and cohesiveness within the immediate or extended family unit. By the second generation, the traditional structure of the family would undergo significant alteration.

The entrance of the United States into World War II offered Oklahoma Mexicans and their American-born children immediate and potential avenues to improve their status and standard of living. Wartime labor requirements forced industries to open new doors to first- and second-generation Mexicans. The practice of defense plants and other war-related enterprises to employ only American citizens encouraged or forced many Mexicans to become naturalized in order to get or keep good jobs. Service in the armed forces was also an easy means of naturalization for those who were not citizens. Mexicans or their children throughout the United States volunteered or were drafted for military service. Many Mexicans from Oklahoma lost their lives in the conflict.

During World War II, Mexican Americans were the nation's most highly decorated ethnic minority. Seventeen Mexican Americans won the Congressional Medal of Honor, including Private First Class Manuel Pérez, Jr., who was born in Oklahoma City in 1923. Private Pérez was a member of the United States Army, Company A, 511th Parachute Infantry, 11th Airborne Division. On February 13, 1945, he led an attack on twelve pillboxes protecting Japanese-held Fort William McKinley on Luzon, Philippine Islands. Using his own rifle, bayonet, grenades, and the rifle of a Japanese soldier he killed in hand-to-hand combat, Pérez single-handedly killed eighteen enemy soldiers and relieved his entire company from immediate danger. Before he received official notification on December 27, 1945, that he had won the Medal of Honor, Pérez was killed by a Japanese sniper. He was later buried in Oklahoma City.[7]

When World War II ended, the Mexican community in Oklahoma faced a period of profound change. The relatively small number of Mexicans in the state was significantly affected by the rapidly changing nature of American society in the postwar period. Children of the immigrants reflected the major impact of that altered situation. They had been born and raised in this country. They had gone to American schools. They spoke English as well as (often better than) they spoke Spanish. They had adopted American customs, and ultimately a large number would marry Anglo spouses. The Mexican community was not large enough to maintain firm cultural roots much beyond the first generation. One of the most significant differences between the Mexican community of Oklahoma and those of the American Southwest was the overwhelming degree of assimilation which the second —and most assuredly the third—generation would undergo in the postwar years.

Chapter 6

THE MEXICAN EXPERIENCE SINCE WORLD WAR II

Oklahomans of Mexican descent entered the postwar period with higher expectations and greater opportunities than ever before. Through service in World War II and later in the Korean conflict, Mexican-American veterans qualified for the "G.I. Bill of Rights." Unprecedented numbers of Mexican Americans in Oklahoma acquired a college education, "on job" training, or loans to establish their own enterprises. They went on to become doctors, lawyers, engineers, accountants, teachers, businessmen, and skilled craftsmen.

Many Mexicans have commented that the postwar period marked the decline, though not the extinction, of the racial prejudice and job discrimination which they had previously experienced. A study conducted in 1949 confirmed that negative stereotyping of and prejudice towards Mexicans did persist in the state. A survey of 1,672 white college students in Oklahoma, Texas, Arkansas, and Louisiana revealed sharp negative attitudes toward Mexicans. The students stereotyped Mexicans as people who possessed low moral standards, would steal, were dirty, helped depress wages, and were lazy and shiftless. Most of these attitudes, they indicated, had been determined through such experiences as family talks, hearsay, classroom discussion, newspapers, and movies. Despite such lingering sentiments, second-generation Mexicans had largely integrated and gained acceptance within the broader culture.[1]

Although first-generation Mexicans usually retained their old ways and remained isolated by language and cultural barriers, the integration of the second generation was almost inevitable. Although they continued to speak Spanish along with English, maintained close family ties, usually married Mexican spouses, and retained a firm awareness of their cultural heritage, second-generation Mexicans were virtually forced into the larger society. The Oklahoma Mexican community comprised an extremely small ethnic minority during and after the war, since most Mexicans left Oklahoma during the depression. Only small cultural islands of immigrants and their children remained in the state. No large *colonias* or *barrios* such as those in the southwestern border states or midwestern urban areas fostered self-sufficient cultural entities. Thus, their small number, limited contact with Mexican culture, use of English, and the absence of segregation and strong overt discrimination promoted integration and often intermarriage.

By the third generation, many Mexican families had undergone nearly complete assimilation. For some young children, Spanish became a language that "mom and dad use to talk to grandma and grandpa." Grandparents noted the tendency of the third generation to marry *"güeros"* and complained that their grandchildren could not speak Spanish. They also lamented that the character of the family had suffered severe alteration in succeeding generations. The *compadrazgo* seemed a relic of but faintly remembered times. One elderly immigrant sadly observed, *"No hay amistad; no hay respeto."* ("There is no friendship; there is no respect [for the older generation].")

Despite the large outflux of Mexicans from Oklahoma prior to World War II, succeeding years have witnessed a gradual increase in the state's Mexican-descent population. A few immigrants from Mexico settle each year in Oklahoma. Mexican-American servicemen who had been stationed at Tinker Field, Vance Air Force Base, Fort Sill, or Altus Air Force Base have remained in the state after completing their enlistment period or retiring. Oklahoma has experienced an important in-migration of Mexican Americans from Texas, particularly from the San Antonio area and the lower Río Grande Valley. Finally, an indeterminate number of undocumented Mexican aliens have migrated to various sections of the state.

Numerically, the most significant of these recent arrivals are those from south Texas, an area which contains one of the largest Mexican-American populations in the United States. The vast majority of these people have worked on large commercial farms, ranches, or small farms in the Valley. Mexican-American families in this region have lived in deplorable conditions for generations. Low wages, unemployment, substandard housing in segregated communities or neighborhoods, poorly funded and equipped schools, and minimal participation in local or state political affairs have characterized their way of life. Most young people drop out of school long before completing high school in order to help support the family. The lack of opportunities for those who do finish school dissuade many more from continuing. For many, Spanish is still their primary language; large numbers are illiterate in English. The scarcity of year-round employment has forced hundreds of thousands of south Texans to migrate each year in search of seasonal work in the north or northwest. The cycle of poverty, low educational attainments, and unemployment has proved to be difficult, if not impossible, to escape.

Until the mid-1960s, many Texas migrants worked the cotton harvest in southwestern Oklahoma. The mechanization of cotton farming at that time, however, greatly diminished the demand for seasonal labor. In the meantime, many had already dropped out of the migrant pool and settled permanently in Oklahoma. They had remained in the state for a variety of reasons. Some stayed to escape the acute prejudice and discrimination they had known in Texas. Others simply tired of the constant traveling and stopped in a community where they could find work on a farm or ranch or in a factory or small business. Once they found permanent employment and began to buy a home, they convinced other family members or friends to come to the state and take advantage of the opportunities it had to offer.[2]

The number and impact of undocumented Mexican aliens in Oklahoma are impossible to determine at present. Mexico's burgeoning population (which is doubling every twenty years), unemployment and underemployment, low wages, and spiraling inflation annually drive millions of *mojados* across the border. Immigration officials presently apprehend and deport approximately one million illegals a year; probably at least an equal number escape detection. While most *mojados* migrate to areas of high Mexican-American concentration in the southwestern border states, many reach Oklahoma. Immigration officials regularly apprehend illegals in Oklahoma City, Tulsa, and elsewhere in the state. The Border Patrol operates a unit on the Will Rogers Turnpike near Miami, Oklahoma, which periodically intercepts *mojados* on their way north and returns them to the border. Between October 1, 1977, and October 31, 1978, immigration officials apprehended 1,268 *mojados* in northeastern Oklahoma alone.

The members of the Mexican-American community in Oklahoma express widely differing views concerning the illegals. Some believe that they depress wages, take jobs from citizens and legal residents, and further burden the social welfare services of the state. Others express sympathy with their plight and believe that regardless of their status in this country, human charity demands that *mojados* receive help when they are in need. Several organizations in the state work with immigration authorities to secure proper papers for those undocumented aliens who qualify for admission to this country. In 1978 a storm of protest arose from the Hispanic community in Tulsa after members of the Tulsa Police Department and immigration officials arrested a number of undocumented aliens near Our Lady of Guadalupe Church. Other arrests took place in business establishments and near a location where a church fiesta was being held.[3]

The decennial census figures illustrate the growth of Oklahoma's Mexican-American population since World War II. The 1950 tabulation indicated 3,501 first- and second-generation Mexicans in the state. The Mexican-stock population reached 4,316 in 1960 and grew to 6,071 in 1970. In 1970 the largest number of first- and second-generation Mexicans lived in Oklahoma City, Tulsa, Altus, and Lawton. The census of 1970 also revealed that 21,843 Oklahomans had been raised in a home where the head or wife considered Spanish the mother tongue. In addition, 51,284 Oklahoma residents identified themselves as persons of Spanish origin or descent. These latter include all persons of Hispanic background, but those of Mexican descent undoubtedly comprise all but a small percentage of that group. Although federal officials admit that the 1970 tabulation grossly undercounted the Hispanic population, the census figures do indicate that a significant number of persons of Mexican descent live in Oklahoma.

The Hispanic population of the state is concentrated principally in the Oklahoma City and Tulsa metropolitan areas and in the southwestern quarter of the state. In 1970 Oklahoma County numbered 15,486 persons of Spanish origin or descent. The vast majority (11,018) lived in Oklahoma City and the surrounding communities of Midwest City (1,609), Bethany (712), Del City (570), The Village (398), Norman (359), and Edmond (353). Tulsa County contained 8,948 Hispanics, including 7,216 in Tulsa, 401 in Sand Springs, and 175 in Sapulpa. Counties in the southwestern portion of the state showing significant Hispanic populations include Comanche (3,031), Caddo (1,967), Jackson (1,906), Carter (1,421), Roger Mills (1,257), Tillman (1,165), Kiowa (668), and Jefferson (661). Some officials estimate that by 1980, the total Hispanic population of Oklahoma may reach 200,000.[4]

Michael M. Smith

A number of organizations presently serve Mexican Americans and other Hispanic residents of the state. These groups oversee the welfare of the Mexican community, encourage participation in civic and religious affairs, promote interest in and appreciation of Mexican culture, and foster social, economic, and educational endeavors. Those groups active in political affairs include the Governor's Advisory Council on Spanish American Relations and the Tulsa Hispanic Commission. Organizations under religious sponsorship include the Archbishop's Commission on Hispanic Affairs and Little Flower Church's Catholic Action Club in Oklahoma City and the Diocesan Hispanic Commission in Tulsa. The Mexican American Cultural Center in Oklahoma City serves as a clearinghouse and coordinating agency for a number of local and state-wide programs and projects affecting the Mexican community. Chapters of the G. I. Forum have been established in Oklahoma City, Elk City, Altus, and Clinton. The Oklahoma Commission on Mexican American Affairs is active in the southwestern counties, while the Oklahoma Rural Opportunities Development Corporation serves many Mexican Americans in agricultural areas. Campus groups include the Mexican American Student Association and the Spanish American Law Students Association at the University of Oklahoma and the Hispanic Community Association at Oklahoma State University. A variety of civic and social groups in Oklahoma City includes the Spanish Speaking Senior Citizens, the Folkloric Association of Mexican Arts, the Mexican American Business and Professional Club, the Pan American Golf Club, the Pan American Women's Club, the Azteca Soccer Club, and Los Amigos Lions Club.

During the 1960s and 1970s, currents of change spawned by the civil rights movement significantly affected Mexican Americans across the United States. While most of the activity was confined to the Southwest, thousands of young Mexican Americans outside the region joined or expressed sympathy for *la causa,* "the movement." Numerous Mexican-American groups were formed to combat discrimination and infringements of civil rights. They also encouraged Mexican Americans to be proud of their rich cultural heritage and sought to promote unity within *la raza,* a concept which includes all members of the Mexican cultural family, north and south of the border. Young activists, rejecting traditional hyphenate status, called themselves *Chicanos* (a truncated form of *mexicano,* which in earlier times had a pejorative connotation) in order to distinguish Mexicans living north of the border from those residing in Mexico.

NUMBER OF OKLAHOMA RESIDENTS OF MEXICAN STOCK, BY COUNTY

1970

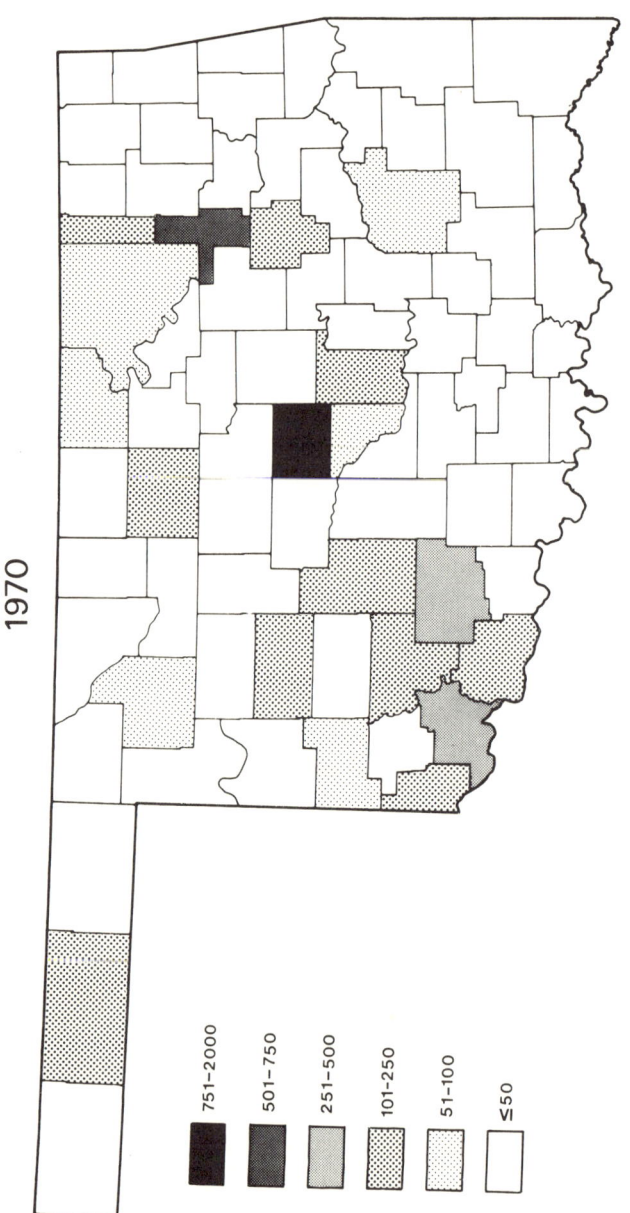

751–2000

501–750

251–500

101–250

51–100

≤50

Source: U. S. Census.

NUMBER OF OKLAHOMA RESIDENTS OF SPANISH ORIGINS OR DESCENT, BY COUNTY 1970

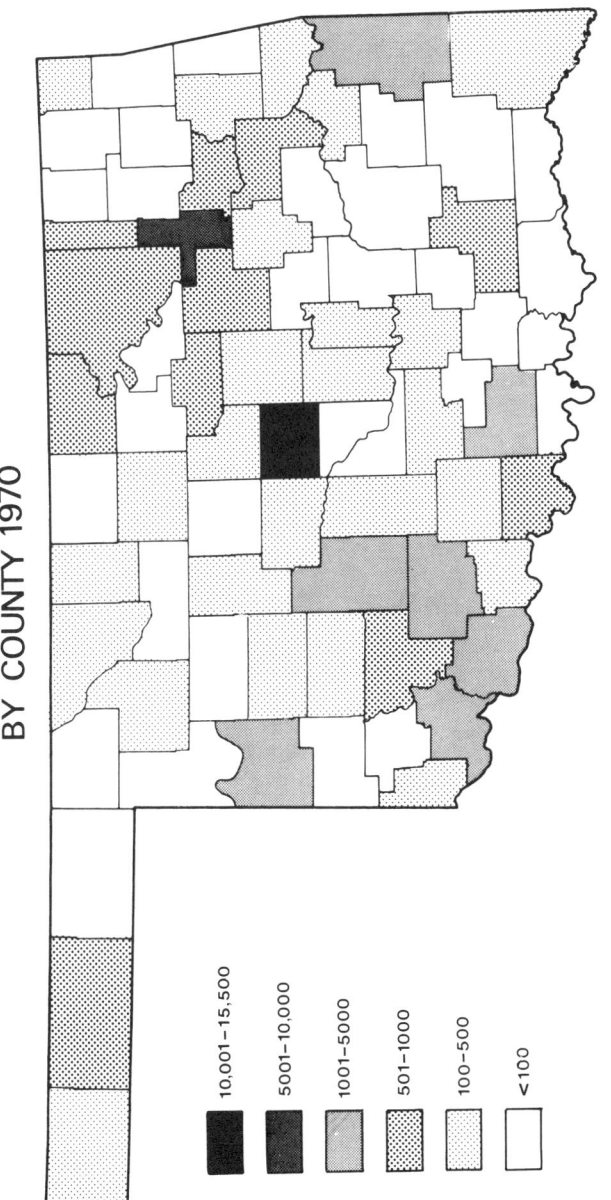

10,001–15,500

5001–10,000

1001–5000

501–1000

100–500

<100

Source: U. S. Census.

A number of Chicano leaders, including César Chávez in California, Reies Tijerina in New Mexico, Rodolfo "Corky" González in Colorado, and José Gutiérrez in Texas, gained national attention. While some activists—notably Chávez—espoused a non-violent approach, many preferred direct confrontation. Numerous strikes, boycotts, demonstrations, and marches led to violent encounters with police, political authorities, and school administrators across the Southwest. Many young Mexican Americans in Oklahoma expressed dissatisfaction with the conservative nature and passivity of the older generation in the state but generally rejected confrontation and chose to work within the system. Most older Mexicans repudiate the designation of "Chicano" (to them it still evokes a strong negative connotation), but the younger generation supports *chicanismo* and its goals.[5]

The cultural pride of the state's older Mexican families, the constant influx of Mexican-American immigrants, and the enhanced consciousness of the Chicano movement have all served to maintain a strong ethnic tradition within Oklahoma's Mexican community. Each year thousands of people throng Oklahoma City's Myriad and the Tulsa Assembly Center to join the "16 de Septiembre" celebrations. Mexican popular music as well as traditional *mariachi* and *ranchera* songs entertain the celebrants. Children in typical Mexican costumes —boys in *charro* suits, girls in *china poblana* dresses—perform traditional dances that their mothers have taught them. Throughout the state, Mexican Americans still observe the Day of the Virgin of Guadalupe with special masses and processions. Each July, Little Flower Church's Catholic Action Club sponsors a fiesta to support its work in the Mexican community. Groups in Oklahoma City, Tulsa, Lawton, and Altus regularly hold dances where bands and performers—often directly from Mexico—entertain with Mexican music and songs. Radio stations in Oklahoma City, Lawton, and Altus schedule weekly Spanish-language programs which feature Mexican music and provide news and announcements of special interest to the Mexican-American community. Mexicans in Oklahoma preserve a living cultural tradition and maintain an abiding sense of ethnic identity.

BIBLIOGRAPHICAL ESSAY

Scholars have ignored the role of Mexicans in Oklahoma. Prior to the present work, no serious study of this immigrant group had appeared. It is hoped that this introductory survey will indicate a need for further research on the topic and encourage others to seek new materials which will give us a more complete understanding of the Mexican experience in Oklahoma. Family records, letters, photographs, and other personal memorabilia will yield valuable clues to the experiences, attitudes, patterns of settlement, occupations, and living conditions of Mexican immigrants. A careful examination of the records of mining and railroad companies, unions, churches, and local and county governments should furnish important data. The most valuable sources of information are the immigrants themselves. Their personal histories will give life to any account of the immigrant experience.

The most readily available printed materials concerning Mexicans in Oklahoma are the decennial censuses, which supply general information on such items as settlement, naturalization, literacy, and language. Unfortunately, there is little data concerning Mexicans in the tabulations of 1890 and 1900, for which the manuscript censuses are now available. The most detailed data concerning Mexicans in the state is the United States Senate, *Reports of the Immigration Commission* [*Dillingham Committee*], vol. 7 (Washington: Government Printing Office, 1911), which examines the Oklahoma coal-mining region. The report provides information concerning years of residence, citizenship, literacy, income, family size, and living conditions. General studies of Mexican immigration and labor, however, mention Oklahoma only in passing, if at all. In sum, nearly everything remains to be done. For those who wish to gain a better understanding of Mexicans, their history, their culture, and their impact, the following selective bibliography is offered as a place to begin.

Any study of Mexicans in the United States must start with an examination of their native land. Hubert H. Bancroft's six-volume *History of Mexico* (San Francisco: A. L. Bancroft and Company, 1883–88) is still a mine of information for the period before Díaz. Ernest Gruening's *Mexico and Its Heritage* (New York: D. Appleton-Century Co., 1934) and Henry Bamford Parkes's *A History of Mexico* (Boston: Houghton Mifflin Company, 1938) are old standards. Lesley B. Simpson's delightful *Many Mexicos* (Berkeley: University of California Press, 1969) is most valuable for its treatment of the colonial period and the nineteenth century. Anthropologist Eric R. Wolf's *Sons of the Shaking Earth* (Chicago: University of Chicago Press, 1959) is an excellent analysis of pre-Columbian Mexico and the interaction between the indigenous and Spanish colonial cultures. Michael C. Meyer and William L. Sherman's *The Course of Mexican History* (New York: Oxford University Press, 1978) is a well-written and finely balanced recent survey.

Works concerning the *Porfiriato* include biographies of the dictator by James Creelman, *Díaz: Master of Mexico* (New York: D. Appleton and Company, 1911); Carleton Beals, *Porfirio Díaz: Dictator of Mexico* (Philadelphia: n.p., 1932); and David Hannay, *Díaz* (London: Constable and Company, 1917). Andrés Molina Enríquez's *Los grandes problemas nacionales* (México: Imprenta de A. Carranza e hijos, 1909) and George McBride's *The Land Systems of Mexico* (New York: American Geographical Society, 1923) discuss agrarian problems during the *Porfiriato*. Leopoldo Zea's *El positivismo en México* (México: El Colegio de México, 1943) is a keen analysis of the major philosophical currents of the period, while John Kenneth Turner's *Barbarous Mexico* (Austin: University of Texas Press, 1969) presents a scathing indictment of the era. Daniel Cosío Villegas's monumental *Historia moderna de México* 9 vols. (México: Editorial Hermes, 1955–70) offers the most complete study of the Díaz regime.

There are numerous excellent books on the revolution. James D. Cockroft's *Intellectual Precursors of the Mexican Revolution, 1900–1913* (Austin: University of Texas Press, 1968) examines early political opponents of the Díaz regime, while Charles C. Cumberland's *Mexican Revolution: Genesis Under Madero* (Austin: University of Texas Press, 1952) traces the initial stages of the revolution. Biographies of central figures include: Stanley R. Ross, *Francisco I. Madero: Apostle of Mexican Democracy* (New York: Columbia University Press, 1955); Martín Luis Guzmán, *Memoirs of Pancho Villa* (Austin: University of Texas Press, 1965); and John Womack, Jr.,

Michael M. Smith

Zapata and the Mexican Revolution (New York: Alfred A. Knopf, 1968). Popular treatments of the revolution include Blanche De Vore, *Land and Liberty: A History of the Mexican Revolution* (New York: Pageant Press, 1966); and Ronald Atkin, *Revolution: Mexico, 1910–1920* (New York: J. Day Company, 1970).

There are numerous works concerning Mexican immigration and labor in the United States. Victor L. Clark's, "Mexican Labor in the United States," *Bulletin of the Department of Labor* 78 (September 1908): pp. 466–522, was the pioneering effort. Other major studies include Paul S. Taylor's ten-part *Mexican Labor in the United States* (Berkeley: University of California Press, 1928–1934), his *A Mexican-American Frontier, Nueces County, Texas* (Chapel Hill: University of North Carolina Press, 1934), and *A Spanish-American Peasant Community: Arandas in Jalisco* (Berkeley: University of California Press, 1933). Mexican anthropologist Manuel Gamio contributed two important works, *Mexican Immigration to the United States: A Study of Human Migration and Adjustment* (Chicago: University of Chicago Press, 1930) and *The Mexican Immigrant: His Life Story* (Chicago: University of Chicago Press, 1931), a collection of personal histories. Cary McWilliams's many studies of Mexican workers include *Factories in the Field: The Story of Migratory Farm Labor in California* (Boston: Little, Brown and Company, 1939), *Ill Fares the Land: Migrant and Migratory Labor in the United States* (Boston: Little, Brown and Company, 1942), and *North From Mexico: The Spanish Speaking People of the United States* (Philadelphia: J. B. Lippincott Company, 1949). Recent works are Abraham Hoffman's *Unwanted Mexican Americans in the Great Depression: Repatriation Pressures, 1929–1939* (Tucson: University of Arizona Press, 1974) and Mark Reisler's *By the Sweat of their Brow: Mexican Immigrant Labor in the United States, 1900–1940* (Westport: Greenwood Press, Inc., 1976). The latest and certainly one of the most important studies of Mexican immigration is Arthur F. Corwin, ed., *Immigrants—and Immigrants: Perspectives on Mexican Labor Migration in the United States* (Westport: Greenwood Press, Inc., 1978).

The development of Mexican-American history as a focus of study is largely a product of the present generation. Valuable works on Mexican Americans include: John H. Burma, *Spanish Speaking Groups in the United States* (Durham: Duke University Press, 1954); Stan Steiner, *La Raza: The Mexican Americans* (New York: Harper and Row, Publishers, 1969); Leo Grebler, Joan Moore, and Ralph Guzmán, *The Mexican American People: The Nation's Second Larg-*

est Minority (New York: The Free Press, 1970); Julián Samora, *Los Mojados: The Wetback Story* (Notre Dame: University of Notre Dame Press, 1971); Ernesto Galarza, *Barrio Boy* (Notre Dame: University of Notre Dame Press, 1971); Feliciano Rivera, *Occupied America: The Chicano's Struggle Toward Liberation* (San Francisco: Canfield Press, 1972); Matt S. Meier and Feliciano Rivera, *The Chicanos: A History of Mexican Americans* (New York: Hill and Wang, 1972); David Weber, *Foreigners in Their Native Land: The Historical Roots of the Mexican American* (Albuquerque: University of New Mexico Press, 1973); and Manuel P. Servín, *An Awakening Minority: The Mexican Americans* (Beverly Hills: Glencoe Press, 1974). Scholarly articles concerning Mexican Americans regularly appear in the *Journal of Mexican American History, Aztlán: International Journal of Chicano Studies and Research, El Grito: A Journal of Contemporary Mexican American Thought,* the *Chicano Law Review,* the *Pacific Historical Review,* and the *Journal of Ethnic Studies.*

NOTES

CHAPTER 1

1. Walter Prescott Webb, *The Great Plains* (Boston: Ginn and Company, 1931), chaps. 2–6; Herbert E. Bolton, *The Spanish Borderlands* (New York: Yale University Press, 1921), pp. 79–119; John W. Morris and Edwin C. McReynolds, *Historical Atlas of Oklahoma* (Norman: University of Oklahoma Press, 1965), pp. 6–11, 15–16, 40; Hugh D. Corwin, *Comanche and Kiowa Captives in Oklahoma and Texas* (Guthrie: Cooperative Publishing Co., 1959).

2. Grant Foreman, *The Five Civilized Tribes* (Norman: University of Oklahoma Press, 1934), pp. 262–66, 336–37; Angie Debo, *A History of the Indians of the United States* (Norman: University of Oklahoma Press, 1970), pp. 113–14; 145–46, 175–77, 260–61; Arrell M. Gibson, *The Kickapoos: Lords of the Middle Border* (Norman: University of Oklahoma Press, 1963).

3. Interview with Robert G. Flanagan, III: 509, Interview with Henry Beaty, XXIX: 131, Indian-Pioneer History, Grant Foreman Collection, Indian Archives, Oklahoma Historical Society, Oklahoma City, Oklahoma; *El Reno News*, 14 September 1899.

CHAPTER 2

1. Arthur F. Corwin and Lawrence A. Cardoso, "Vamos al Norte: Causes of Mass Mexican Migration to the United States," in *Immigrants—and Immigrants: Perspectives on Mexican Labor Migration to the United States,* ed. Arthur F. Corwin (Westport: Greenwood Press, Inc., 1978), pp. 38–41.

2. Among the best general studies of Mexico are: Charles C. Cumberland, *Mexico: The Struggle for Modernity* (New York: Oxford University Press, 1968); Michael C. Meyer and William L. Sherman, *The Course of Mexican History* (New York: Oxford University Press, 1979); Lesley Byrd Simpson, *Many Mexicos* (Berkeley: University of California Press, 1969); and Eric Wolf, *Sons of the Shaking Earth* (Chicago: University of Chicago Press, 1959).

CHAPTER 3

1. Manuel Gamio, *Mexican Immigration to the United States* (Chicago: University of Chicago Press, 1930), pp. 13–29.

2. Corwin and Cardoso, "Vamos al Norte," pp. 40–44.

3. George O. Coalson, "The Development of the Migratory Farm Labor System in Texas: 1900–1954" (Ph.D. diss., University of Oklahoma, 1955), pp. 24–26; Gamio, *Mexican Immigration*, pp. 23–29; Arthur F. Corwin, "¿Quien Sabe? Mexican Migration Statistics," in *Immigrants—and Immigrants: Perspectives on Mexican Labor Migration to the United States*, ed. Arthur F. Corwin (Westport: Greenwood Press, Inc., 1978), pp. 109–10; Lawrence L. Waters, "Transient Mexican Agricultural Labor," *Southwestern Social Science Quarterly*, 22:1 (June 1941): 49–66.

4. Victor S. Clark, "Mexican Labor in the United States," *Bulletin of the Department of Labor* 78 (September 1908): 469–74.

5. Larry G. Rutter, "Mexican Americans in Kansas: A Survey and Social Mobility Study, 1900–1970" (M.A. thesis, Kansas State University, 1972), pp. 29–44; Clark, "Mexican Labor," pp. 474–76.

6. Corwin and Cardoso, "Vamos al Norte," p. 52; Corwin, "¿Quien Sabe?," pp. 110–14; Interview with Miguel González, Lawton, Oklahoma, 23 April 1979.

7. Rutter, "Mexican Americans in Kansas," pp. 40–41; U.S., Congress, House, *Interstate Migration of Destitute Citizens: Hearings before the Select Committee*, Oklahoma City Hearings, 19–20 September 1940, 76th Cong., 3rd sess. (Washington: Government Printing Office, 1941), pt. 5, pp. 1799–1807.

8. Corwin, "¿Quien Sabe?," pp. 115–17.

9. U.S., Department of the Interior, Census Office, *Twelfth Census of the United States Taken in the Year 1900: Population* (Washington: Government Printing Office, 1901), I, pt. 1, pp. 734–49.

10. U.S., Department of Commerce, Bureau of the Census, *Thirteenth Census of the United States Taken in the Year 1910: Population* (Washington: Government Printing Office, 1913), III, pp. 461, 466–79, 483.

11. U.S., Department of Commerce, Bureau of the Census, *Fourteenth Census of the United States Taken in the Year 1920: Population* (Washington: Government Printing Office, 1923), III, pp. 815, 827; *Daily Oklahoman*, 20 May 1921.

12. U.S., Department of Commerce, Bureau of the Census, *Fifteenth Census of the United States: 1930: Population* (Washington: Government Printing Office, 1932), III, pt. 2, p. 573.

13. U.S., Department of Commerce, Bureau of the Census, *Sixteenth Census of the United States: 1940: Population* (Washington: Government Printing Office, 1943), II, pt. 5, pp. 857–59.

14. Interview with Gregorio Martínez, Oklahoma City, Oklahoma, 22 February 1979.

CHAPTER 4

1. U.S., Congress, Senate, *Reports of the Immigration Commission*, VII: *Immigrants in Industries*, pt. 1: *Bituminous Coal Mining*, 61st Cong., 3rd. sess. (Washington: Government Printing Office, 1911), p. 16 (hereafter cited as *Bituminous Coal Mining*).

2. Samuel Bryan, "Mexican Immigrants in the United States," *The Survey*, 28 (September 1912): 726–30; Clark, "Mexican Labor," p. 477.

3. Interview with Simeón Urende, Oklahoma City, Oklahoma, 27 February 1979; Interview with Sofía Urende, Oklahoma City, Oklahoma, 27 February 1979.

4. Clark, "Mexican Labor," p. 496; M. Ganley, "Characteristics of the Mexican,"

Railway Age Gazette, 53 (September 1912): 529; L. J. Hughes, "Good Treatment Necessary for Mexicans," *Railway Age Gazette,* 53 (September 1912): 528-29, Rutter "Mexican Americans in Kansas," p. 81; James P. Craig, "How to Handle Mexican Labor," *Santa Fe Employees Magazine,* 8 (November 1914): 27-29.

5. Rutter, "Mexican Americans in Kansas," p. 77.

6. L. C. Lawton, "Erecting Mexican Laborers' Houses," *Santa Fe Employees Magazine,* 5 (September 1911): 75-76.

7. Interview with Aurora Ramírez Helton, Tulsa, Oklahoma, 18 April 1979; Interview with Jack Helton, Tulsa, Oklahoma, 18 April 1979.

8. Frederick L. Ryan, *The Rehabilitation of Oklahoma Coal Mining Communities* (Norman: University of Oklahoma Press, 1935), pp. 25-49.

9. *Bituminous Coal Mining,* pp. 16-41.

10. Philip A. Kalisch, "Ordeal of the Oklahoma Coal Miners: Coal Mine Disasters in the Sooner State, 1886-1945," *Chronicles of Oklahoma,* 48 (Autumn 1970): 331-33; *Bituminous Coal Mining,* pp. 69-70.

11. *Bituminous Coal Mining,* pp. 41-59.

12. Ibid., pp. 65, 71-88.

13. Ibid., pp. 16, 89-126.

14. Interview with Heginio Casillas, Tulsa, Oklahoma, 27 March 1979.

15. Unidentified and undated newspaper clipping, Barde Collection, Oklahoma Historical Society, Oklahoma City, Oklahoma.

16. *Daily Oklahoman,* 18-21 December 1929; *McAlester News-Capital,* 17-23 December 1929; Kalisch, "Ordeal of the Oklahoma Coal Miners," p. 338.

17. Ryan, *The Rehabilitation of Oklahoma Coal Mining Communities,* pp. 61-76, 89; Interview with Heginio Casillas; Interview with Agustín Romero, Broken Arrow, Oklahoma, 24 March 1979; Interview with Dolores Romero, Broken Arrow, Oklahoma, 24 March 1979.

18. Clark, "Mexican Labor," pp. 467, 476.

19. Charles E. Webb, "Distribution of Cotton Production in Oklahoma: 1907-1962" (M.A. thesis, University of Oklahoma, 1963), pp. 9-11; Clark, "Mexican Labor," p. 471; Ramsen Crawford, "The Menace of Mexican Immigration," *Current History,* 31:5 (February 1930): 904; Paul S. Taylor, *Mexican Labor in the United States: Dimmit County, Winter Garden District South Texas* (Berkeley: University of California Press, 1930), p. 457; Interview with Petra Martínez, Lawton, Oklahoma, 23 April 1979; Interview with Guadalupe Nieto, Tulsa, Oklahoma, 7 April 1979; Interviews with Simeón Urende, Sofía Urende, Agustín Romero, Dolores Romero, Gregorio Martínez, Miguel González, Aurora Ramírez Helton, and Jack Helton.

CHAPTER 5

1. Unless otherwise noted, the information for this chapter was derived from interviews with Petra Martínez, Guadalupe Nieto, Simeón Urende, Sofía Urende, Agustín Romero, Dolores Romero, Gregorio Martínez, Miguel González, Aurora Ramírez Helton, Jack Helton, and Heginio Casillas.

2. Clark, "Mexican Labor," p. 498.

3. Matt S. Meier and Feliciano Rivera, *The Chicanos: A History of Mexican Americans* (New York: Hill and Wang, 1972), p. 148.

4. Paul S. Taylor, "Songs of the Mexican Migration," in *Puro Mexicano,* ed.

J. Frank Dobie (Dallas: Southern Methodist University Press, 1935), pp. 221–45.

5. Manuel Gamio, *Mexican Immigration,* pp. 132–34, 242–45.

6. The author wishes to thank Louis Scagnelli, O.C.D., and John Michael Payne, O.C.D., of Oklahoma City for information concerning the Discalced Carmelites in Oklahoma. Additional information concerning the order's work may be found in various issues of *The Little Flower Magazine.*

7. U.S., Congress, Senate, *Medal of Honor Recipients, 1863–1978.* Committee on Veterans' Affairs, 96th Cong., 1st sess. (Washington: Government Printing Office, 1979), pp. 652–53.

CHAPTER 6

1. Eugene S. Richards, "Attitudes of College Students in the Southwest Towards Ethnic Groups in the United States," *Sociology and Social Research,* 35:1 (September-October 1950): 22–30.

2. Group discussion with Paul Leyja, Silvia Torres, Raymond Coronado, María Coronado, Sister Silvia Negrete, and Father Ward Darnell, Frederick, Oklahoma, 22 April 1979; Interview with Sister Kathleen Blanchard, Tulsa, Oklahoma, 19 April 1979.

3. *Tulsa Tribune,* 9 November 1978.

4. U.S., Department of Commerce, Bureau of the Census, *United States Census of Population: 1950.* IV, *Special Reports,* pt. 3, chap. A, *Nativity and Parentage.* (Washington: Government Printing Office, 1954), p. 3A–77; U.S., Department of Commerce, Bureau of the Census, *United States Census of Population: 1960. Subject Reports. Nativity and Parentage.* Final Report PC(2)–1A. (Washington: Government Printing Office, 1965), p. 151; U.S., Department of Commerce, Bureau of the Census, *Census of Population: 1970.* I, *Characteristics of the Population,* pt. 38. (Washington: Government Printing Office, 1973), pp. 158, 163, 205–207, 268–70, 311–17.

5. For an example of literature concerning the Chicano movement, see Rodolfo Acuña, *Occupied America: The Chicano's Struggle Toward Liberation* (San Francisco: Canfield Press, 1972).